CUT
DEAD
BUT STILL
ALIVE

CUT DEAD BUT STILL ALIVE

CARING FOR AFRICAN AMERICAN YOUNG MEN

Gregory C. Ellison II

Abingdon Press
Nashville

CUT DEAD BUT STILL ALIVE
CARING FOR AFRICAN AMERICAN YOUNG MEN

This book is printed on acid-free paper.

Library of Congress Cataloging-in-Publication Data

Ellison, Gregory C., II.
    Cut dead but still alive : caring for African American young men / Gregory C. Ellison II.
        pages cm
    ISBN 978-1-4267-0304-1 (book - pbk. / trade pbk. : alk. paper) 1. African American youth—Social conditions. 2. Social service—United States. I. Title.
    E185.86.E437 2013
    305.2350896'073—dc23

                                                        2013006714

Scriptures taken from the Holy Bible, New International Version®, NIV®. Copyright © 1973, 1978, 1984, 2011 by Biblica, Inc.™ Used by permission of Zondervan. All rights reserved worldwide. www.zondervan.com.

Poems on pages xx, 48, 72, 106, and 136 are copyright © 2013 by William K. Gravely. All rights reserved. Used by permission.

13 14 15 16 17 18 19 20 21 22—10 9 8 7 6 5 4 3 2 1

MANUFACTURED IN THE UNITED STATES OF AMERICA

CONTENTS

ACKNOWLEDGMENTS

Several years ago in a small church in rural Georgia, a wise woman told me that the "longest journey you will take in life is the trip from your head to your heart." In penning the words for this book, I challenged myself to embark on this journey and meld my intellectual interests with my most creative sensibilities and heartfelt passions. On this journey I occasionally met resistance. However, a community of reliable others planted, cultivated, and nurtured seeds of hope within me and encouraged me to be my authentic self. It is because of their collective prayers, encouraging words, constructive criticism, and midnight musings that *I am* in a position to offer these words of gratitude. Therefore, I find it most fitting to begin this book on the muted and invisible by *acknowledging* those who have given me hope, visibility, and voice.

While on this journey, a host of mentor-teachers encouraged me to uncover pockets of freedom and creativity within the disciplinary boundaries of academia. I am especially grateful for the wise tutelage of Drs. Robert Dykstra, Donald Capps, Brian Blount, Geddes Hanson, Peter Paris, Kenda Dean. Each shepherded me through the hilly regions and marshlands of Princeton Theological Seminary. Of equal recognition are my colleagues at Emory University's Candler School of Theology who offered support and direction as I carved out a path for myself as a first-time author. To Drs. Emmanuel Lartey, Karen Scheib, Luther Smith, Bobbi Patterson, Teresa-Fry Brown, Andrea White, Arun Jones, Ellen Ott-Marshall, Ian McFarland, and my colleagues from the New Directions Conference, I offer special thanks. Finally, I lift up the pedagogues who sparked the embers in my imagination and encouraged me to use my pen as a pillar of fire to guide me through the dark night of the soul. For this I extend heartfelt gratitude to Drs. Jacqueline Jordan Irvine, Johnnetta B. Cole, Maisha T. Winn, Howard Thurman, Cheryl Talley, Dorothy Simpson, Sharon Fluker, John Kutsko, and Kathy Armistead. Of equal note are Professors Mari Evans, James Brown, Anthony Earnest, Luciano Pereira da Silva, Michael Thompson, Amy Benson Brown, Deborah van der Lande, Brenda Roberts, and Arramando Kawai.

So, too must I recognize the host of individuals who have sojourned with me at different points on this pilgrimage. Their timely advice to push forward, rest, celebrate small accomplishments, and, above all, remain grounded has made this expedition to see more clearly and hear more acutely memorable and worthwhile. For their companionship and love, I express heartfelt thanks to the Simpson, Ellison, Watts, Greenaway, Rollins, Dixon, and Day families. In the moments when I lost my way, the families of Leslie Washington, Neil Rollins, Rodney Francis, Jonathan Walton, Josef Sorett, Audrey Thompson, Kenyatta Gilbert, Dwight and Kenya Davis, Cedric Grant, Rodney Shamery, Lerone Martin, Luke Powery, Matthew Williams, Stephen Lewis, Lawrence "Torry" Winn, De Amon Harges, Garnesha Crawford, Delvecchio Finley, Rahiel Tesfamariam, Akpovogho Igherighe, Peter Altmann, and James Logan erected signposts to set me back on course; thank you. Worthy of note are the beloved institutions that sheltered me with loving hospitality and nursed me back to health while ailing on this trek— The Fund for Theological Education, The Louisville Institute, Memorial West Presbyterian Church (Newark, New Jersey), Concord Baptist Church (Brooklyn, New York), Impact Church (Atlanta, Georgia), St. James United Methodist Church (Kansas City, Missouri), and Mt. Zion Baptist Church (Boonton, New Jersey).

On this expedition from head to heart, I am grateful for the classes of students at Candler, Sewanee, CCCG, the Institute of Youth Ministry, the W. E. B. Du Bois Summer Scholars Institute, and Uth Turn, who pressed me to cut through the thick underbrush of traditional standards of research, writing, and teaching. On these strategic diversions, I learned to hear the voices in the wilderness and see hope within the shadows. To my surprise, whenever I found myself deep in the forest, wearied and seemingly alone, emerging from a clearing were my research assistants, Michael Slack, Christina Repoley, Michelle Ledder, Brandon Maxwell, Reginald Wilborn, Marita Harrell, and Mario Stephens, much obliged.

Acknowledgments

Chief among the lessons learned on this pilgrimage was the immense power of fearless dialogues. I am honored to carry with me the stories of young leaders I met in my three years at the W. E. B. Du Bois Summer Scholars Institute at Princeton University. For thirteen months at Uth Turn, a juvenile reentry program for young men leaving correctional facilities, I was privileged to "sit at the feet" of nearly two hundred young men, hearing both tragic stories and narratives of hope. So, too, I am humbled to hold the stories of countless students close to my heart. To be sure, this book would lack intensity and punch if Nathaniel, Art, Thomas, Stephen, Carl, and William K. Gravely had not allowed me to walk with them into the luminous darkness of their stories in search of timeless wisdoms. The stories of these courageous young men will illumine the hearts and minds of caregivers who strain to see and hear those who have been cut dead. The weight of these stories called me to be more honest with myself and write without fear.

It goes without saying that time away on pilgrimage fosters a greater appreciation of home. However, on this journey from head to heart, I have come to realize that home is not a physical place. Home is understanding. The following individuals relieved my homesickness. To the cloud of ancestral witnesses that beckoned me to write for the unnamed and the unborn, ashe and shalom. Bernard Kynes, whose modestly confrontational presence created a safe space for me to vent, cry, and process my frustrations, for you I pray shalom. Toby Sanders, professor, counselor, brother, friend, I love you, shalom. Gregory, Sr., Jeannette, and Darren, who saw me first as son, brother, and friend, I love you, shalom. Antoinette, my final stair, confidante, and dearest love, I love you, shalom. Elisha Alexander, my guardian angel, you continue to teach me to appreciate the moment for the morrow is not promised, I love you, shalom. Greg III, your smile in the morning gives me hope for the day, and your kiss at night gives me promise for the future, I love you, shalom. Anaya Kaira, my wise teacher, your gentle compassion and careful discernment route me home when I find myself between seemingly disparate worlds, I love you, shalom. To the Reliable Other, I am because I AM, I love you, shalom.

INTRODUCTION

Unwavering, the legs of the bridge stand firm. But the road beneath has a life of its own. Like beleaguered lungs gasping for air, the road moves up and down with the vibration of passing vehicles. Mimicking a fading heart, the road emits a pronounced "thump-thump" as speeding cars hit divots every few seconds. Perhaps this road seems alive because at the foot of the bridge, just steps away from traffic, a tall, wiry six-foot-four man lies, cut dead. Vital fluids cascade from the crown of his head, and a warm pool of blood steams on the cold concrete like molten lava.

As the sun sets, a crowd gathers in two concentric circles around the crumpled body. The shadow-cast faces are indistinguishable, but their mouths move as they speak in muted tones. In the inner circle stands one with a garish knife wound to the neck; to his left, one with a furrowed brow and callous eyes; and to his left, one with a much shorter silhouette, a gun protruding from his pocket. Steps away from the crumpled corpse, the murky blood inches closer to another young man's burgundy wingtips. Weary, he drops three dictionary-sized books to the ground, and blood spurts onto his shoes and pinstriped slacks. Completing this inner circle of young African American men stands one whom I learned they called "Holiday." Huddled in the outer circle, a reliable band of caregivers—teachers, parents, activists, ministers, counselors, and scholars—strain to see through the darkness and hear beyond the steady roar of passing traffic.

The Inner Circle

Each of the young men in the inner circle has a story and a once-envisioned hopeful future. However, at some point in their journey, they felt unseen and unheard, and their future hopes began to wane. Before jumping off the bridge, Stephen was a nationally ranked athlete and local celebrity. Carl, the young man who slit his throat, spoke Japanese fluently. Nathaniel's furrowed brow carried years of stress, for he functioned as the primary caretaker of his younger sisters. In his pinstripe suit and wingtips, Art excelled in school at every level. But after the "incident," he slept in class. Thomas, an infamous gang leader, wanted to alter his path and attend college, but he could not escape his criminal record and the reputation of his former life as "Holiday." As for the unnamed young man with the gun, his future lies in wait.

Although the scene under the bridge did not actually happen, it is a composite blending of real-life stories. This book chronicles the lives of these six African American young men between the ages of fifteen and twenty-four. It argues that the muteness and invisibility they experienced forecloses possibilities for a hopeful future by threatening four fundamental human needs: control, self-esteem, a sense of meaningful existence, and belonging.[1] These dangerous threats had not gone totally unnoticed, however.

The Outer Circle

In the opening vignette of this chapter, a cast of caregivers surrounding the six young men strains to see and hear. Comprised of relatives, ministers, scholars, and community members, this group of caregivers stands in solidarity with and in support of the young men in crisis. However, there is an uneasy distance between the two circles. These caregivers are peering over the shoulders of the inner circle and seek greater access to better understand the gifts and needs of the young men.

This distance from the inner circle creates angst for many well-intentioned caregivers who jockey for the right space, position, and ideology to connect with unacknowledged groups in authentic ways. To be sure, a few caregivers may gain physical access to inner circles occupied by African American young men, but these caregivers may still sense an emotional gulf. Recognizing this mixture of benevolent intentions and uneasy distance, this book offers theoretical tools and practical strategies to care with marginalized populations.

This book garners "expert" wisdom from therapeutic conversations drawn from case studies. It highlights best practices from master practitioners in counseling, ecclesial settings, and various community agencies that maneuver this uneasy territory to care for those on the margins. The study speaks to scholars with distinct disciplinary perspectives on the ill effects of being unacknowledged and the nature and power of human hope.

In full self-disclosure, years ago, *I* stood in the inner circle, feeling muted and invisible but surrounded by a community of reliable others. Now as a thirty-five-year-old caregiver, I stand on the outer rim. I peer over the shoulders of African American young men, and I struggle to hear their voices and see them more clearly. To fully liken my own experiences of muteness and invisibility to those of African American young men twenty years my junior would be unwise. However, in the chapters that follow I can and do speak authoritatively about the tensions I felt as a caregiver moving between worlds, offering care in marginal places, yet still reckoning with my own issues of visibility and voice. In short, this text views the investigator's insights (my insights) as instrumental to this study. This method of including the researcher's involvement as intrinsic to the investigation counters the principles of scientific objectivity that govern "rigorous" research. However, I am not the first practical theologian to accentuate the relationship of theory and praxis. Pioneering pastoral psychologist James Dittes also believed that controlled use of the investigator's own experience can make "results both more meaningful and more reliable."[2] It is my hope that the inclusion of my "I" moving from the outer-circled caregiver into the inner-circled world of the muted and invisible is enriching and informative.

The Traffic

In the fictive account that begins this chapter, cars whizz by a gathered crowd and grant little attention to an unfolding crisis. In the hurried traffic of our daily routine, how many people do we snub completely and deliberately ignore? The primary role of the caregiver is to see that which is overlooked and to hear that which is not spoken. Attentive seeing and listening requires not being consumed by the endless traffic occupying our daily calendars but becoming hyperattentive to persons and communities hidden in plain view.

Caregivers must have "ears that hear and eyes that see—the LORD has made them both" (Proverbs 20:12). But do we see the people who maintain the grounds of our campus, empty the trash at our office building, and operate the cash register at the local fast-food chain? Do we hear the concerns of abused children, battered wives, the youth in the balcony of our church, or the gifted international student reluctant to speak in class? Even more hidden are the concerns of the seemingly powerful. Do we see the wealthy business-woman who commands respect in the office but is little more than a pinion in the eyes of her family? Do we hear the silent tears of the ever-smiling, positive-minded megachurch pastor, surrounded by beloved parishioners, none of whom he can trust? We need not look only to jails, senior-citizen centers, or inner-city park benches to find the muted and invisible, for the unacknowledged are all around us, but we must sharpen our vision and at-tune our hearing to care.

From years of learning to see more clearly and hear more acutely, I recog-nize that having one's body, voice, and psyche go unnoticed in public space and discourse is a problem that extends beyond race, class, or culture. How-ever, it has also become clear to me that African American males between the ages of fifteen and twenty-four are particularly susceptible to the detrimental effects of *muteness* and *invisibility.* This population of young men is substan-tially at risk of being muted and made invisible as a result, in part, of fewer opportunities for higher education, disproportionate rates of incarceration, resistance to counseling and therapeutic introspection, dehumanizing por-trayals of African Americans throughout history and in the modern media, and shame-laden interpretations of the physical body and human sexuality in American history and Christian pedagogy.

Ironically, while African American young men are particularly suscepti-ble to muteness and invisibility, an alternate image exists of the hypervisible African American male in modern media. This strange juxtaposition leads to my hypothesis that the intense and exclusive one-dimensional focus on young African American male entertainers and professional athletes further perpetuates the silencing and exclusion of the masses of African American young men. For instance, many young African American athletes in the me-dia are often characterized as lacking the ability to think critically and make educated decisions, while some entertainers are presented as prizing material wealth over communal empowerment. Though these characterizations may be accurate at times, they are not normative, for there are also socially pro-gressive, community-minded African American male athletes and entertain-ers who receive considerably less attention. Such a monolithic view amplifies the stereotypes that make muteness and invisibility possible, and it leads potential caregivers to speed by persons in crisis with indifference, fear, or scorn.

Though this book specifically aims to offer strategies to clearly see, hear, and care for muted and invisible young men, more broadly it seeks to widen the horizon of all who give care. How we choose to see or not to see and to hear or not to hear those around us speaks to our ability to identify the presence of God in others. Biblical wisdom tells us that the good Samaritan has been labeled "good" throughout the annals of time because he suspended judgment and left the traffic of his daily routine to see, hear, and care. Caring with unacknowledged and marginalized populations requires altered vision and altered pace. This work is not for the faint of heart. I must caution readers: once you see, you cannot *not* see.

The Road Ahead

In this book, I examine the lives of several African American young men and frame the therapeutic conversations with them as case studies that highlight how young African American men are silenced, rarely seen, and made vulnerable by a lack of sustained introspection. Most of these therapeutic conversations derive from my work with African American high-school and college-aged students from various churches and institutions of higher learning, as well as with young men transitioning from juvenile detention centers and prisons at Uth Turn correctional services in Newark, New Jersey. Although each of the young men chronicled has granted me permission to share his story, to ensure their anonymity, pseudonyms are used. The small sample size may concern some. But there is no monolithic African American experience,[3] and the young men mentioned in these case studies are representative of the complexity of geographic, socioeconomic, and educational diversity among African American young men.[4] Additionally, the case studies highlight the lengths to which some young men will go to be seen and heard and the tragic consequences of decisions made when they are denied visibility and voice. Inherent in these case studies, though less noticeable to the inattentive eye, is the presence or absence of a community of reliable others who can aid these young men in finding hope, visibility, and voice.

This book examines the scholarship of theorists from distinct disciplinary perspectives who have variously considered the ill effects of muteness and invisibility and the restorative nature and power of human hope. These theoretical sources also address the challenges faced by caregivers who confront the complexities of navigating narrative, time, and space. Further, the insights of these interdisciplinary theorists are employed to offer strategies to establish rapport and embolden hope among marginalized populations.

The first chapter, "Cut Dead," defines the problem of muteness and invisibility and makes a case for a strategic pastoral theological response. The chapter begins by charting the long and sordid history of literature and psychological theories connected to muteness and invisibility. After defining key terms, various interdisciplinary theories are used to frame a lack of acknowledgment as a potential impediment to hope and primary threat to what social psychologist Kipling Williams calls the four fundamental human needs: control, self-esteem, a sense of meaningful existence, and belonging.[5]

The second chapter outlines parameters to guide pastoral theological theory and practice for caregivers working with unacknowledged populations. Subdivided into four sections, the chapter focuses intently and separately on the four words *caring with marginalized populations*. These subsections examine four approaches to care, the fluidity of marginality, issues of critical distance, and the caregiver's wholeness.

Chapters 3 through 6 are each structured around a fundamental human need that is deadened by muteness and invisibility and a caregiving strategy to enliven hope. Chapter 3, "The DEATH of Control and the BIRTH of Fearless Dialogue," examines the loss of control and "boundary-breaking" interpretive strategies that give voice to those who are muted. Chapter 4, "The DEATH of Self-Esteem and the SEED of an Interrupting Hope," analyzes the power of an interrupting hope to disrupt the loss of self-esteem and foil the woeful ills of despair, apathy, and shame. Chapter 5, "The DEATH of Meaningful Existence and the BIRTH of Miraculous Solutions," examines Solution-Focused Brief Therapy, a novel therapeutic perspective that vitalizes meaning in life by reframing time and envisioning new possibilities. The final chapter, "The DEATH of Belonging and the Life-Giving COMMUNITY of Reliable Others," uncovers the crippling effects of isolation and proposes an action plan for caregivers to sustain and generate hope through acknowledgment and accountability.

Fearless dialogue, an interrupting hope, the search for miraculous solutions, and the presence of a community of reliable others represent four primary resources that diminish the ill effects of being unseen and unheard. These resources equip previously unacknowledged African American young men to face difficulties, envision new possibilities, and work proactively toward change. The four primary resources also aid caregivers in navigating between disparate worlds, retaining hope in seemingly hopeless situations, and confronting personal and professional risks.

A Final Word on Circles

It is no coincidence that this introduction began with a dying young man at the center of two concentric circles. In closest proximity to this center stood a cast of African American young men who each felt his hope threatened by a lack of acknowledgment. At the edges of the inner circle, a group of caregivers gathered around these young men and peered over their shoulders. In the midst of this chaotic moment and in the setting of the "Golden Day," traffic passed on the periphery.[6]

From start to finish this book places African American young men, often deemed as marginal and powerless, at the center. In no way are their voices censored. Their storied lives are mined as sites of wisdom with the power to inform generations of students and caregivers about how to care effectively. Although marginality is not valorized, it is framed as a site of resistance where hope is born and change is catalyzed. In an effort to highlight the possibility of change from the margins and to complement the case studies of once muted African American men, a poem by William K. Gravely introduces five of the six chapters. William is a twenty-five-year-old spoken-word artist and recent seminary graduate who laid down his pistol for a pen. His poems chart his own evolution and expose the gritty realities of an African American young man who is cut dead but is still alive and struggling for hope. Along with the case studies, these poems open a door into a world that some of us could otherwise not imagine.

Like William Gravely, I view my own movement from the inner circle of unacknowledged youth to the outer circle of caregivers artfully. My freewheeling style of writing—that moves from poetry and prose to cultural criticism and historical snapshot—reflects the artistic and pragmatic approach of a liminal caregiver who treks back and forth from margin to center. This style of writing also authentically embraces the instrumental quality of my role as investigator and uses my lens to bring additional clarity to the problems of muteness and invisibility. Finally, the creative writing in this book mirrors my approach to teaching and counseling, which maintains that facilitators must capture the audience's imagination in seconds, else these facilitators find themselves tuned out and invisible.

The paradigm of this book couches caregivers between the center and the margin. Huddled near the circle of young men, caregivers stand in close proximity to care fully, making themselves susceptible to receiving unfiltered and unbridled rage. Likewise, these same caregivers buffer these young men from the calloused indifference and scornful gaze of passing traffic, knowing that these outside sources (like the academy, church, or surrounding community) can slaughter the caregiver's reputation and livelihood for taking such a stance. Yet, you and I, as caregivers, choose to embrace these risks and move between the center circle and the traffic to enliven hope and care with those cut dead but still alive.

Invisible Assumptions

See me? I know you're lookin'! . . . but in your
eyes I'm just a hoodlum

If that's all you choose to see, that's all I choose
to be

Why waste time tryin' to climb out of this box
you built for me

'Cause at least in a casket I'll be viewed and
seen,

I lived as a ghost, and accomplished the most,
my imprisoned mind could dream

—William K. Gravely

CHAPTER ONE

CUT DEAD

Spared from the gallows of emptiness and impotent despair, the fortunate human soul finds life and the potential to flourish when noticed favorably by others. However, some living souls endure the woe of being passed over with no account. Like phantoms, they ache to be seen and heard. But, persistent unacknowledgment takes a toll on their psyches. With shadow-cast faces, they teeter from explosive rage to implosive depression. Locked in an unending nightmare, their future hopes diminish, and the daily existence of facelessness becomes a cruel and fiendish torture. Herein lie the stories of the faceless phantoms, tramping through city streets, suburban corridors, and college campuses, screaming from the shadows to be seen and heard. They are the *cut dead but still alive.*

Cut dead is a nineteenth-century idiom meaning to be ignored deliberately or snubbed completely. In 1896, the noted American psychologist William James employed this phrase in the tenth chapter of *The Principles of Psychology.* James argued that humans are social with an innate desire to be noticed, and noticed favorably, by others. Conversely, going unnoticed or being cut dead is torturous:

> No more fiendish punishment could be devised, were such a thing physically possible, than that one should be turned loose in society and remain absolutely unnoticed by all the members thereof. If no one turned around when we entered, answered when we spoke, or minded what we did, but if every person we met "*cut us dead*," and acted as if we were nonexistent things, a kind of rage and impotent despair would before long well up in us, from which the cruelest bodily torture would be a relief.[1]

James's description of being cut dead expresses the inner torment, indignation, and potential social threat of persons who feel categorically unseen and unheard. Decades after James's account on the torment of being cut dead, the African American mystical theologian Howard Thurman echoed a similar sentiment.

A grandson of slaves, Thurman knew well the anguish of utter disregard. In a meditation entitled "A Strange Freedom," his words reflect the unyielding psychological duress of going unnoticed:

> It is better to be the complete victim of an anger unrestrained and a wrath which knows no bounds, to be torn asunder without mercy or battered to a pulp by angry violence, than to be passed over as if one were not. Here at least one is dealt with, encountered, vanquished, or overwhelmed—but not ignored. It is a strange freedom to go nameless up and down the streets of other minds where no salutation greets and no sign is given to mark the place one calls one's own.[2]

Like James's portrayal of the cut dead, Thurman's strange freedom yearns for favorable attention to prevent internal dissipation. The unnamed protagonist in Ralph Ellison's *Invisible Man* takes a different approach. Instead of inner corrosion, he demands notice at all costs.

Beyond the turmoil of being nameless, Ralph Ellison's protagonist illustrates the lengths taken by the unacknowledged to be seen and heard. With the aching need to know he exists in a world that continually overlooks him, the narrating protagonist reports:

> To convince yourself that you do exist in the real world, that you're a part of all the sound and anguish, you strike out with your fists, you curse, and you swear to make them recognize you. And alas, it's seldom successful.[3]

The weighty toll of striking out with words and fists for mere recognition describes yet a fraction of the psychological toll of living a cut-dead existence.

In these three accounts we find internal turmoil and externalized rage. On one hand, James's and Thurman's strangely free souls seek to avoid the internal anguish of being cut dead. On the other hand, we hear of Ralph Ellison's protagonist flailing violently in desperation to be seen and heard. The cut dead but still alive vacillate between the ravaging throes of internal ruin and external destruction.

To make the case that African American young men are particularly susceptible to the tortuous effects of being cut dead, this chapter examines the fragmenting portrayals of this population in statistical data, sensational propaganda, and sociological studies. The chapter concludes with a social-psychological paradigm of ostracism that identifies how the perils of muteness and invisibility threaten four fundamental human needs. However, in order to set the context, this chapter begins with a concise definition of muteness and invisibility.

Cut to the Chase: Muteness and Invisibility Defined

I refer to being unheard and unseen as *muteness* and *invisibility*. Consider these terms individually. In short, *muteness* alludes to silencing. In certain instances, outside forces silence and render a person mute. But, muteness may also take shape as an internal silencing, in which actions or emotions are contained, repressed, and not expressed in speech or vocal utterance. In other words, muteness is an incapacity or unwillingness to verbalize that which is present within.

Most literally, *invisibility* refers to "that which by nature is not an object of sight."[4] However, in *Invisible Man,* Ralph Ellison connects invisibility to the unexamined life. In an interview about the protagonist's invisibility, Ralph Ellison explains:

> The major flaw in the hero's character is his unquestioning willingness to do what is required of him by others as a way to success . . . He goes where he is told to go; he does what he is told to do; he does not even choose his (own) name. It is chosen for him and he accepts it. The hero's invisibility is not a matter of being seen, but a refusal to run the risk of (knowing) his own humanity.[5]

More than not being visible to the naked eye, invisibility is also the complicit acceptance of a limiting identity and the failure to risk the required self-scrutiny to know one's own humanity.

External and internal pressures fuse together muteness and invisibility. External forces such as media propaganda, government policies, and historical prejudices have the power to render people and communities silent and seemingly unworthy of being seen. Not removed from these external pressures, internal forces wreak havoc within the psyche, leading some people and communities to believe their words are worthless, their presence meaningless. In the unacknowledged person's war between the self and the system, the critical introspection necessary for change and the development of hope wanes. Working in tandem, external and internal pressures create a sense of muteness and invisibility that contributes to a physical and psychological sense of non-acknowledgment of body and voice. Findings show that striving for visibility and voice begins early in life, unfortunately to no avail for some African American boys.

Cut-and-Dry: Statistical Evidence of Muteness and Invisibility

What does it mean to be a black man? Imagine three African American boys, kindergarteners, who are largely alike in intelligence, talent and character, whose potential seems limitless. According to a wealth of statistics and academic studies, in just over a decade one of the boys is likely to be locked up or headed to prison. The second boy—if he hasn't already dropped out—will seriously weigh leaving high school and be pointed toward an uncertain future. The third boy will be speeding toward success by most measures.

—Michael A. Fletcher, *Washington Post*

On Friday, June 2, 2006, those staggering numbers headlined in the *Washington Post*, launching a month-long series of articles entitled "What Does It Mean to Be a Black Man?" Three months prior to the *Post's* series, *The New York Times* featured an article on its front page titled "Plight Deepens for Black Men, Studies Warn." In this article, Erik Eckholm summarized key findings in *Black Males Left Behind*, an edited volume of essays from leading researchers around the country who have studied the effects of poor education on young African American men who are increasingly disconnected from mainstream society. With the emergence of the Trayvon Martin case, discussed later in this chapter, national scrutiny of the plight of African American men continues.

Consider the pronounced educational deficits of African American young men. In 2010, 47 percent of black men versus 78 percent of white men graduated from high school. Additional data from the Bureau of Labor Statistics shows that among the sixteen- to twenty-four-year-olds surveyed, 64.9 percent of black students did not attend college, compared with 57.8 percent of white students. These educational statistics point to a variety of difficulties for young black men.[6] Most apparent is the fact that a lack of education adversely affects one's opportunities.

Less evident in these statistics are the struggles of the young African American men who don't fall through the cracks. In 2010, of the 48.7 percent of black students who graduated from high school, 50.2 percent remained unemployed.[7] And what is to be said of the 35.1 percent of young African American students between the ages of sixteen and twenty-four who do pursue a college education? What tools will they employ to be acknowledged in a sea of faces that look different from theirs? Will the lack of positive African American male role models on college campuses lead them down the slippery slope of disgust and despair?

According to figures from the Bureau of Labor Statistics, college-educated black men, especially, have struggled to find gainful employment in the economic downturn: "The unemployment rate for black male college graduates 25 and older in 2009 has been nearly twice that of white male college graduates—8.4 percent compared with 4.4 percent."[8] An earlier essay by Harry J. Holzer, Steven Raphael, and Michael A. Stoll in *Black Males Left Behind* supports this phenomenon and suggests that despite their educational attainment, the stigma attributed to young black men as potential criminals stifles their ability to attain gainful employment. Holzer and colleagues note that because many employers fear hiring criminals, and they either cannot afford or are unwilling to screen for criminal involvement, these employers "take the easy way out and simply refuse to hire blacks as a proxy for keeping crime out of their shops."[9] Thus, regardless of educational attainment, African American young men are subject to stigmatizing forces that render them mute, invisible, and susceptible to despair.

In a study conducted by the Justice Policy Institute, Princeton sociologist Bruce Western explains that "for low-education African American men, prison has become a common life event, even more common than employment or military service." Through assessment of Bureau of Justice statistics, Western predicted that "29% of African American males born in 1991 will spend some time in prison in their lifetime."[10] Western's grim predictions have become reality as more than 846,000 African American men filled prison cells in 2008, numbers of them between the ages of eighteen and twenty-five.[11] These statistics reveal how disproportionate numbers of young African American men's physical bodies are (and will be) rendered invisible to society through incarceration and how their voices are (and will be) rendered mute in public discourse through unemployment and a lack of education.

But though these statistics provide a useful quantitative tool to assess and predict the potential life outcome for African American young men, they fail to reveal how these young men are seen or not seen by society and how they choose to see or not see themselves. A look at historic portrayals of black men coupled with a critical examination of current media depictions will show how and why African American young men may be cut dead by the general public, and even by the caregivers who seek to do them no harm.

Cutting Lines: Headlines, Timelines, Flatlines, and the Black Male Body

On February 26, 2012, while walking home a seventeen-year-old African American young man named Trayvon Martin was gunned down by an over-zealous neighborhood watchman who thought the young man looked suspicious. Martin, who shielded his head from the evening rain with a hooded sweatshirt, was armed only with a pack of Skittles candies and a can of iced tea. Weeks after his death, Trayvon Martin became a household name, Skittles and hoodies emerged as cultural icons, and groundswell movements of protest made national news. In this firestorm of media frenzy, I was invited to lead a workshop on muteness and invisibility on the campus of Atlanta's Morehouse College, the nation's only all-male historically black institution of higher education.

On an unseasonably warm March afternoon, a dozen Morehouse men filed into the workshop. Just steps from the classroom window, students milled around in the muggy conditions donning hooded sweatshirts. In less than an hour, many Morehouse men would gather on the steps of the Georgia State Capitol with throngs of other placard-toting, Skittles-carrying collegians protesting the wrongful death of seventeen-year-old Trayvon Martin. While the mood of the hoodie-wearing students corralled outside reached a fever pitch, tempers also began to boil in our climate-controlled classroom. Our conversation on "invisible assumptions" held by modern media coverage of tragedies such as Trayvon's would be far from tempered.

Headlines

With little introduction, the workshop participants were broken into small groups and given five minutes to conduct cursory headline news research on a given name. Transfixed before smart-phone and laptop screens, the students read the stories of black men whose lives had been cut short or altered from being cut dead. Some students were disgusted and enraged, and others showed signs of confusion or indifference. When time elapsed, the students shared the following five accounts:

- In 1997, New York City police arrested **Abner Louima** in a citywide crackdown on crime and sodomized him with a broken broom handle during interrogation. Louima's sodomy attack prompted widespread anti-police brutality rallies throughout New York.

- Two years later, four plainclothes police officers cornered **Amadou Diallo**. When Diallo pulled out his wallet to show identification, the officers unloaded their weapons and shredded his body with forty-one gunshot wounds. Diallo's death sparked national cries and fiery protests against racial profiling.

- Ten years after Diallo's murder, in Chicago, sixteen-year-old honor student **Derrion Albert** found himself caught in the crossfire of a brawl between two rival factions when walking to the bus stop after school. Albert was sideswiped by a wooden railroad tie, knocked unconscious, and beaten until lifeless. His last living moments were captured on a crude cell-phone video and broadcast on syndicated news and Internet sites. Rallies and public statements by government officials followed.

- In 2011, at a house party less than thirty miles from Morehouse's campus, the college-bound **Bobby Tillman** crossed an invisible barrier into a world of unceasing rage. Unexpectedly hit, Tillman fell to the ground and was stomped mercilessly until a bone punctured his heart. His killers had never before seen his face. Posthumously, town-hall meetings were held, and anti-bullying campaigns sprang up on social media.

- The fifth headline story was more difficult to track. In fact, few traces of the incident could be found on the Internet. Like the other cases, the senseless killing spurred anti-violence marches and generated media frenzy in metropolitan Atlanta. However, seventeen years after he was pinned to the ground and shot after a rival basketball game, **Brandon Williams**'s name is nearly untraceable.

After hearing these headlines, with little prompting, students began making connections between the sensational media coverage and public outcry in Trayvon Martin's case and the five other news stories. The students felt that the melodramatic headlines and media coverage of these tragedies induced fear and fascination in the public imagination and tarnished the image of all young black men. Speaking of this fear and fascination, one student suggested that for some viewers newscast coverage of slain black bodies may evoke the same intrigue, fear, and awe as watching predators devour prey on the Discovery Channel. This student's analogy pinpoints the historic pains of black males living in the tensions of public spectacle and private scorn.

Timelines

Through the timelines of American history, propaganda has fashioned the black male body as alluring and forbidden; erotic, but fearsome. After the Civil War and Reconstruction, stereotypes arose that portrayed African Americans as hypersexual and equated their personhood (or the lack thereof) with their genitalia and sexual exploits. These dominant myths depicted African American men and women either as threatening creatures with the potential for sexual power over whites or as harmless, desexed underlings of a white culture.[12] Two such stereotypical images of African American men grew to mythic proportions, producing both fantasy and fear in white America: the sexually threatening and violent "black buck" and the apparently docile Sambo.

The black buck was conceived as a complementary image to that of the typecast promiscuous black woman. African American males were portrayed by white culture as "wild, bestial, and violent bucks."[13] The black buck evolved into a monstrous image of the African American male as a sexual aggressor who preyed on innocent white women. Perceived as a threat to society, the black buck could only be tamed in slavery through physical brutalities such as whipping, castration, or lynching.

In contrast to the black buck was the Sambo, framed as a trusted confidante of the master or mistress. The Sambo caricature was viewed by the dominant culture as a happy, docile, domesticated servant. The Sambo stereotype was supposedly asexual and posed little to no threat to his master. These contrasting mythic images presented African American men as distorted, dehumanized creatures whose bodies distinguished them from the white norm of beauty, further subjecting them to inhuman treatment.

Unfortunately, the archaic tropes of the black buck and Sambo still permeate modern media portrayals of African American young men. One need not look far to find fearmongering representations of African American men in the media. Whether it be a gun-toting rapper flanked by scantily clad lingerie models or mug shots of Troy Davis, executed in 2011 for the alleged murder of a Georgia police officer, images of modern-day black bucks flicker and flash across digitized screens. Due to the incendiary consequences of labeling specific individuals as Sambos, I refrain from naming African American men in this category. However, debate continually swells over box-office hits that feature black male actors in self-deprecating roles. Clearly, stereotypes of African American men that evoke fear and fascination remain detectable decades after their origin.

Most problematic is the fact that stereotypic representations of black bodies in the media have power to influence the court of public opinion regarding the worth or worthlessness of African American young men. I am reminded of the dated, yet timeless, example of Robert Mapplethorpe's nationally recognized artistic depiction of African American male bodies, exhibited in the 1980s. Lauded for his technical and aesthetic compositions, Mapplethorpe constructed his images around race, sexuality, and desire. Many of his portraits highlight and focus on the anatomy—genitalia, chests, and buttocks— of African American men. For instance, in his piece "Man in Polyester Suit," an African American man is presented "without a head, wearing a business suit, his trousers unzipped, and his fat, long penis dangling down, a penis that is not erect."[14] In reflecting on the pretext and mixed motives of "Man in Polyester Suit," Mapplethorpe biographer Patricia Morrisroe comments that in their initial meeting, Mapplethorpe was "smitten" with Milton Moore, the photographed model. Mapplethorpe's "love/obsession with Moore reached its fullest expression" in the aforementioned photograph, which many consider to be Mapplethorpe's defining work.[15] Even if the artwork was developed out of love, and the artist did not intend to present a degrading image, his depiction of the African American male body is morbidly problematic because the oversized penis takes priority over the person's (absent) head. Without a face, the person is not whole, and "the penis becomes the identity of the Black male."[16] Mapplethorpe's image of the beheaded African American male body captures and perpetuates the one-dimensional perspective from which African American men historically have been seen as physically and sexually threatening without the capacity to reason and think.

Faceless and headless in the eyes of their killers, the hooded Trayvon (2012) and wallet-brandishing Diallo (1999) were presumed guilty and perceived as criminally threatening. The college-bound Derrion Albert (2009) and Bobby Tillman (2011) were slain by the hands of black teenagers fashioned in the media as merciless savages. Perhaps these summaries sound overstated, but unconscious historic stereotypes color the pages of these headline stories. And the stereotypes promote flat, one-dimensional renditions of human life that heighten fear. These invisible, historically rooted assumptions streaming through media outlets amplify public distrust and make the process of cutting dead a young black man admissible under the guise of personal safety. Shockingly, even caring professionals monitoring flatlines internalize these death-dealing assumptions.

Flatlines

One might think caregivers—those most concerned with the plight and invested in the flourishing of the unacknowledged—would find themselves exempt from deleterious, invisible assumptions. But perhaps the caregivers closest to the despair of the muted and invisible are those most susceptible to these assumptions. John A. Rich, an accomplished physician, public health practitioner, and professor of health management and policy at Drexel University, who has devoted decades to caring for African American young men in trauma units, suggests that even the most well-intentioned caregivers are not immune to holding crippling stereotypes.

In *Wrong Place, Wrong Time: Trauma and Violence in the Lives of Young Black Men*, Rich unfolds the stories of injured young black men teetering on the brink of death and of the health professionals who nurse them back to life. In charting the recoveries of these young men, Rich became acutely aware of his own prejudgments and the malignant perceptions of African American young men held by many health professionals in an inner-city Boston hospital. Rich indicts himself and the trauma specialists around him of carrying an invisible and "unspoken assumption":

> When a young black man rolled into the emergency room with a gunshot wound, we all assumed that it wasn't just bad luck. He didn't just get shot; he got himself shot. This assumption was confirmed in the murmurs that followed the patient's departure from the trauma suite. The ER team cleaned themselves up and washed their hands with a kind of disgusted satisfaction. Sure, they did their job and saved a life. But they were pretty sure, lacking evidence or information to the contrary, that they had saved the life of a drug dealer, gangbanger, or some other stereotype of a young black male absorbed from the news or television.[17]

These telling words reveal that caregivers must remain conscious that they, too, are vulnerable to the same unconscious stereotypes held by the rest of the world. To assist caregivers in checking stereotypic assumptions, Rich proposes the development of a common language that values humanity. Recognizing the power of language to humanize, chapters 4 and 6 of this book examine the components necessary to promote shared meaning and view the previously unacknowledged as "experts" of their own story. To fully understand the problem, we must delve even deeper into social structures that strip the cut dead of humanity by unduly categorizing them as potential criminals, Social dynamite, and Social junk.

Cut Short: Criminalblackman, Social Junk, Social Dynamite, and Explosive Rage

Like the eerie calm before the storm, silence filled the room after the Morehouse men heard the final headline. With the stunning intensity of a lightning bolt slicing through the silence, I posed the striking question, "Who's missing?" A downpour of responses filled the room: Sean Bell, Emmitt Till, Brandon White, the Jena 6. Then, like rolling thunder in the distance, a baritone voice rumbled, "I'm missing!" The levees broke. Tension flooded the room as the deep voice boomed, "He's missing . . . and he's missing . . . and he's missing." In a moment of unfiltered emotion, we tapped the visceral heartache of living a stigmatized existence. Then, the silence returned.

The *Oxford English Reference Dictionary* defines *stigma* as "a mark or sign of disgrace or credit."[18] Though a person may receive some form of social credit from being stigmatized, stigmas are largely viewed as unjust signifiers of a person's or group's character and identity. More often than not, stigmatized people are viewed as "flawed, compromised, and somehow less than fully human."[19] Forced to carry such negative connotations, stigmatized people represent a departure from what is normative and thus are subject to social avoidance and rejection. The stigmatized are also targets of prejudice, hatred, and physical threat. Consequently, psychologists believe the major effect of stigmatization is not the physical threat that the stigmatized endure, but the psychological stressors that are part of their daily existence.[20] Stigmatized people live with the threat of being treated prejudicially, are more prone to confront daily hassles by the law, and are more liable to face limits on their access to resources such as health care, housing, education, and employment. Three socially constructed stigmas that imperil the daily existence of African American young men are those of the "criminalblackman," social junk, and social dynamite.

Criminalblackman

The student's admission that, but for the grace of God, he and any other scholar in that room could have populated the list of headlines uncovers a somber reality that at any moment, even the brightest and most promising African American young man can be cut dead. Sociologist Michelle Alexander, author of *The New Jim Crow: Mass Incarceration in the Age of Color Blindness,* posits that in a culture of mass incarceration, "young + black + male" is the archetypal figure of the "criminalblackman" who at any time can be subjected to terror:

One need not be formally convicted in a court of law to be subject to this shame and stigma. As long as you "look like" or "seem like" a criminal, you are treated with the same suspicion and contempt, not just by police, security guards, or hall monitors at your school, but also by the woman who crosses the street to avoid you and by the store employees who follow you through the aisles, eager to catch you in the act of being the "criminalblackman."[21]

Based on his admission that he, too, could be headline material in a tragic circumstance, the baritone-voiced student likely knew intimately of this archetypal reality.

Alexander argues that the criminalblackman archetype is a by-product of an age of perceived color blindness in which explicit talk of race as a justification for discrimination, exclusion, and social contempt is taboo. Instead, the criminal justice system labels people of color as "criminals" and then engages in exclusionary practices seemingly left behind in the mid-twentieth century.[22] In the era of the New Jim Crow, the criminalblackman ideology "justifies the arrest, interrogation, search, and detention of thousands of African Americans every year, as well as their exclusion from employment and the denial of educational opportunity."[23] Once processed and possessing a criminal history, persons are siphoned into what Alexander calls the system of mass incarceration. In this system, "criminals" not only are locked behind actual bars in actual prisons but also find themselves "behind virtual bars and virtual walls—that are invisible to the naked eye but function nearly as effectively as Jim Crow laws once did at locking people of color into a permanent second-class citizenship."[24] Fixed in the position of second-class citizenship, those branded as criminals are marked by a permanent social exile that complicates attaining housing, gaining meaningful work, and attaining credit, and that generates contempt and scorn not just from employers and social workers but also from neighbors, teachers, and family.[25]

Key to Alexander's portrayal is the thin line of demarcation between the "criminalblackman" and the person actually processed as a criminal. With the former, the person need not possess any criminal history but only "look like" or "seem like" a criminal to be a target of prejudice, hatred, and physical threat. In the latter group are those with actual criminal records who may find themselves subjected to social avoidance and rejection in all facets of life. In either instance, the social stigma of perceived or actual criminality disgracefully marks African American young men and places them in physically threatening and psychologically stressful situations. To be sure, African American young men handle the stressors of dehumanizing stereotypes and stigmatization differently, but I have found that many slip and slide along the continuum between enraged explosion and psychic implosion.

Social Junk and Social Dynamite

Sociologist Christian Parenti aptly describes the dilemma faced by many ambitious African American young men seeking acknowledgment and striving for success. Referencing criminologist Steven Spitzer's article "Toward a Marxian Theory of Deviance" in *Lockdown America*, Parenti divides cast-off populations into two categories: "social junk" and "social dynamite." "Social junk" are people of feeble mind and body whose lives have deteriorated and whose spirits have shattered. Within this group, Parenti includes the homeless, the mentally ill, drug addicts, alcoholics, and the forgotten elderly. Because their spirits are broken and their futures are bleak, they generally pose no immediate threat to the social order other than the fact that they are deemed less than aesthetically pleasing.[26]

The other half of this "dispensable" population is "social dynamite." This group presents a greater challenge to the social order because it is unpredictable and volatile. Social dynamite are characterized as "impoverished low-wage working class and unemployed youth who have fallen below the statistical radar."[27] In contrast to social junk, social dynamite are considered a volatile population because their spirits are not completely broken, and they strive for and expect to attain a decent life and social inclusion.[28] The term *dynamite* suggests that this population is a volatile ticking time bomb waiting and wanting to blow up. Closer examination reveals that, like dynamite used to carve out the side of a mountain, the dynamism of this population and their willingness to create a new reality are inherently constructive. However, constructive potential lessens as boundaries and limitations mount.

Unlike social junk who have succumbed to hopelessness, social dynamite desire a better situation. Their impoverished and stigmatized state becomes more frustrating as they fully view the spectacle of the prosperity of those in power. In their quest to achieve a better life, social dynamite must face not only poverty but also the myths, stereotypes, and stigmas that prevent their full social inclusion.

Though social junk pose no immediate threat to society, they have the potential to raise a flag in the minds of those in power, signaling that the economic system is not properly functioning. Since social junk are perceived as "eyesores," authorities drive them away from the park benches and shopping areas of resort towns, airports, and other pleasure zones.[29] Due to the perceived danger that social dynamite present to communal order, they are controlled differently from their stigmatized counterparts. Parenti notes:

> Controlling [social dynamite] requires both a defensive policy of containment and an aggressive policy of direct attack and destabilization. They are contained and crushed, confined to the ghetto, demoralized and pilloried in warehouse public schools, demonized by lurid media, sent to prison and at times dispatched by lethal injection or police bullets. This is the class—or more accurately the caste, because they are increasingly people of color—which must be constantly undermined, divided, intimidated, attacked, discredited and ultimately kept in check with what [Frantz] Fanon called the "language of naked force."[30]

According to these categorizations, social junk pose no immediate threat to society and are discarded. Social dynamite are deemed more volatile due to discontent with their stigmatized status and limited opportunities and thus are strategically contained. Based on the claims about how stigmatized populations are controlled, one could argue that African American young men who are rendered invisible possess the attributes of both social junk and social dynamite.

Using Parenti's terms, African American young men who have become depressed from years of stigmatization and subjugation to the pressures of life can be categorized as social junk. A by-product of this depression is relinquishing one's ability to fight for change; instead of confronting others, the individual injures himself. Such resignation and self-injury may contribute to substance abuse and poor decision-making because one has lost sight of one's goal and has given up hope that fighting the social structures that create demeaning stigmas will make any difference in one's life outcome. An example of this "junk" among African American young men, on the one hand, may include the high-school student who never learned to read. After years of being labeled "dumb" and "slow," he becomes disinterested in school. As Gravely might say, this young man resigns himself to the fate of "not wasting time tryin' to climb out of this box" of stigmas built for him. With little hope of attaining viable employment because of literacy issues, he may use drugs as a means to escape stigmatizing voices and the pressures of life.

An African American young man who might be characterized as social dynamite, on the other hand, would be filled less with depression than with disgust. Unlike the self-injury of the depressed, the disgusted project their displeasure outward toward particular people and institutions.[31] When dreams for acknowledgment and a better condition are threatened, disgust-prone African American young men sometimes seek inclusion and decency through confrontational routes. In the case of a high-school student who never learned to read proficiently, as a result, he begins to "act out" and is labeled a troublemaker. In the eyes of many, this young man is "just a hoodlum," and even the most perceptive teacher might fail to notice that his poor conduct is a reflection of disgust—with his reading limitations, the potential stigma of being called "dumb," and of his frustration with not performing at the level of his peers.

Further analysis of the depressed high-school student labeled as social junk and the disgusted student categorized as social dynamite reveals one prominent common denominator. Both stigmatized individuals realize, on some conscious or unconscious level, that their social identity has been devalued, making it more difficult for them to attain their desired goals.[32] Though both stigmatized populations are discontented with how they are identified, I argue that social dynamite are more hopeful than social junk, in that their disgust with their predicament fuels them to fight to attain their goal of social inclusion and a decent life "by any means necessary." On the other hand, social junk can be seen as less hopeful, as they have resigned themselves to the fact that their future is blocked.

At some point in their lives both social junk and social dynamite had dreams that were thwarted, promises that were broken, and opportunities that were closed. Do the social dynamite have more willingness to fight to achieve their goals merely because they have not lived long enough with limited possibilities? Were the social junk once social dynamite who have now become too burdened to continue to dream? At some point, those in each group strove to have their humanity acknowledged, but was that humanity recognized, discarded, or contained? African American young men slip and slide along this continuum, a claim readily substantiated in countless individual stories and statistics.

16

One final analysis addresses the misperception that the stigmas of social junk and social dynamite are limited to those of lower socioeconomic status. In this regard it is necessary to consider that social controls to contain or discard stigmatized groups are inflicted at all levels of socioeconomic strata, regardless of academic background and credentials. For example, consider the lives of upwardly mobile minorities hired for positions within companies that lack ethnic diversity. In these circumstances, if the minority is outspoken and opinionated, he might be labeled as a radical and be isolated so as not to upset the status quo. Similarly, a minority who is less outspoken might be pegged as lacking ambition and, in turn, may be viewed as easy to discard. Because this book chronicles the lives of African American young men in impoverished communities with little education as well as students at elite institutions of higher education, it is of vital importance to recognize that many of these young men can be identified at some point on the spectrum between social junk and social dynamite. On the latter end of the spectrum, there exists a dynamic power for personal and communal change: rage.

Explosive Rage[33]

What happens to a dream deferred? . . .
*does it **EXPLODE**?*

—Langston Hughes, "Harlem"

Dynamite's exploding. He has been ready to for a while now. With hopes unseen and dreams unheard, he sees few other options for visibility and voice. Now, all see, hear, and feel his rage.

Though society tends to collapse the two, rage is more than an intensification of anger. Such a shallow analysis reduces rage to a fleeting pathological emotion, and not the spiritually endowed healing force of change. In *Killing Rage*, bell hooks distinguishes rage from anger by analyzing a scene from Toni Morrison's seminal work, *The Bluest Eye*. hooks notes that the novel's narrator believes the dehumanized and colonized little black girl, Pecola, will find hope only if she can express her rage. Speaking of Pecola's plight, the narrator tells readers, "anger is better [because] there is presence in anger." For hooks, presence demands visibility, and it surfaces when the colonized express rage.[34] When presence and the desire to be seen emerge,

17

anger ceases and rage takes over. In this regard, rage empowers the muted and invisible to mobilize and to seek visibility and voice at all costs.

The dynamism of rage must not be viewed solely as a violent force. Such a view would be far too reductionist. Rage, like dynamite, can be used productively. For instance, dynamite can be employed as a destructive weapon to cause great harm. The same stick of dynamite can be harnessed and constructively used to create new pathways by carving out the side of a mountain. The channeled rage of muted and invisible African American young men holds great possibility for personal and communal change.

Transformative rage is paradoxical because rage is borne out of brokenness, but its ultimate aim is wholeness. The progression to wholeness is clarified by further distinctions between rage and anger. While anger stagnates and stews, rage acknowledges a deficit and intensely pursues a remedy.

In trying to make sense of her own rage, bell hooks arrives at the realization that rage has an inclination to heal. She states: "My rage intensifies because I am not a victim. It burns in my psyche with an intensity that creates clarity. It is a constructive healing rage."[35] hooks suggests that truncating rage into limiting categories of temporal, disorganized violence diminishes its liberative power. Viewed more expansively and theologically, transformative and liberative rage transcends even the desire for visibility. In its purest sense, rage seeks full acknowledgment of one's being as having been made in the image of the Divine. Many black male bodies denied visibility and voice become enraged because a spiritual matter inside them conveys a different message. This spiritual voice within tells them that there exists a place above and beyond this one where matters of seeing are left to the One who saw all first. Black men are depleted, and rage is their outcry. This world must start to listen (or these explosions may start looking for victims).

***

In sum, each of these studies describes the dynamics of dysfunction that impair the visibility and voice of African American young men. The examination of tragic headlines, the origin of stereotypes, and the susceptibility of well-intentioned caregivers to hold prejudices highlight the social challenges besetting African American young men seeking visibility and voice. Alexander's and Parenti's studies identify the threats to human flourishing when persons are categorized as criminal, social junk, or social dynamite. However, hooks offers hope that raging dynamism can be healing and productive. In tandem, these texts connote that lack of acknowledgment affects the self holistically. To conclude this chapter, I employ social psychology to more fully examine just how muteness and invisibility attack the whole person by threatening four fundamental human needs.

Cut Down to the Core: Social Psychology and the Human Need for Recognition

Animals who are ostracized inevitably face an early death. They are ostracized by their pack for being mentally or physically ill, or for any other behavioral displays that may threaten the survival of the group. Once ostracized, they lack the resources to capture and secure their food, no longer do they enjoy the protection of their group, and are prevented from forming bonds that provide social sustenance. They lag behind, become decimated, and eventually die through malnutrition or from attack.

—Kippling D. Williams, *The Social Outcast*

Biologists, psychologists, and psychotherapists have long understood that social recognition promotes healthy development, while being unseen and unheard threatens thriving. John Bowlby, most noted for his pioneering work in attachment theory, concluded that the human infant needs a secure relationship with adult caregivers, not only for basic survival, but also for healthy emotional and physical development. Akin to William James equating being cut dead to cruel punishment, psychotherapist Alice Miller suggests in *Breaking Down the Wall of Silence* that children receiving the silent treatment from authority figures is possibly the most sadistic form of child abuse.[36] In *Life History and the Historical Moment* and *Identity, Youth and Crisis*, developmental theorist Erik Erikson argues that interpersonal interaction is essential for psychosocial development, and the lack of such interaction can be detrimental to psychological growth.[37] In *Challenging Invisibility*, pastoral theologian Karen Scheib chronicles the lives of several elderly women who question the meaningfulness of their lives after being rendered invisible by their churches, families, and communities.[38] In sum, being cut dead is a pernicious threat to psychological development at any stage of the life cycle.

A new generation of psychology scholars has further explored race and invisibility. In *From Brotherhood to Manhood: How Black Men Rescue Their Relationships and Dreams from the Invisibility Syndrome*, Anderson J. Franklin, the Honorable David S. Nelson Professor of Psychology at Boston College, reports that the invisibility syndrome in African American men "is an inner struggle with feeling that one's talents, abilities, personality, and worth are not valued or recognized because of prejudice and racism."[39] Valerie Purdie-Vaughns and Richard Eibach, psychology professors at Columbia University and the University of Waterloo respectively, have extended scholarship on this lack of acknowledgment by exploring concepts of "intersectional invisibility." In their study, Purdie-Vaughns and Eibach assert that people with multiple marginalized identities (e.g., ethnic minority, woman) are more likely to experience acute social invisibility and its ill effects of misrepresentation, disempowerment, and further marginalization.[40] Social psychologist Kipling D. Willliams's voluminous studies on social ostracism are of most import for this study on muteness and invisibility in African American young men.

In *Ostracism: The Power of Silence,* Williams traces the ubiquity of ostracism across cultures and times. He charts the range of exclusion from formal declarations of government-sanctioned exile, religious shunning, and military-imposed silencing to short time-outs imposed by teachers, unexplained silences, and averted eye contact in close interpersonal relations. These studies examine the impact of the immediate, short-term, and long-term effects of being excluded and ignored on both the targets and the sources of ostracism. The crucial contribution of this text, however, is Williams's taxonomic model of ostracism and the innumerable case studies that give ostracism a face and transform this intellectually abstract concept into an everyday reality. Consider two such cases that will illustrate how ostracism attacks fundamental human needs.

First, *Ostracism* challenges us to simply remember rather than imagine:

Recall for a moment a situation in which your friends, family, coworkers, or relationship partners acted as though you did not exist. Remember feeling as though you were invisible, yet you could see the others going about their lives as though nothing unusual was happening. What did you do? Did you try talking to them to find out what was going on? But what if they didn't talk back, but instead acted as though they had not heard you? Maybe you waved your hands in front of their faces? If you did, what did it feel like when they looked right through them and you? What did you think when they even refused to make eye contact with you? Were you able to carry on as though everything was normal? Did you start to withdraw? Or did you reciprocate their actions? Remember the time your family or friends made plans and everyone was included except you? Did you ask to be involved anyway, or did you disengage, wondering if you really belonged with these people anyway?[41]

Williams takes a well-calculated risk that every person has experienced an episode of ostracism in some form.

While the first example helps locate the reader as a formerly ostracized person, the second example draws us into the world of an average high-school student, who very well could be our neighbor, relative, or friend. In an in-depth interview, this teenage girl describes the cruelty and inner torment she experienced after being given the silent treatment by her schoolmates:

At one stage they refused to speak to me for 153 days, not one word at all. This was a very low point for me in my life and on the 153rd day [of being ostracized by my classmates], I swallowed 29 Valium pills. My brother found me and called an ambulance. When I returned to school [after overdosing on Valium], the kids had heard the whole story and for a few days they were falling over themselves to be my friend. Sadly, it didn't last. They stopped talking to me again and I was devastated. I stopped talking myself then. I figured that it was useless to have a voice if no one listened.[42]

Although this case does not feature African American young men, Williams broadens our understanding of the sheer cruelty of being cut dead. Sustained attacks of muteness and invisibility eroded this young woman's sense of self to the point that she attempted to permanently mute her voice with twenty-nine Valium pills. She was literally cut dead. Found by her brother, she was given a second chance at life, only to be cut dead again. She then found her voice useless and chose not to speak. Might there have been other alternatives to stay alive? This question is all too familiar for the young men chronicled in this book, who grasp for new opportunities to live and hope, again only to be cut to the point of death.

Williams's two cases exemplify the varied responses to being muted and invisible. The first vignette of remembering a moment of ostracism conjures up a bevy of self-probing questions on how to regain control and to refocus on purpose and whether to reconnect with the person(s) denying visibility and voice. These queries and the subsequent actions are short-term responses to going unacknowledged. The second example, however, reveals the torment of long-term ostracism. In the case of the high-school student, the prolonged lack of connection threatens her self-esteem, heightens her feelings of helplessness, and challenges the belief that her existence is worthwhile.[43] Hopeless and disconnected, she swallows twenty-nine pills. Whether ostracism is short and intensive or long and extensive, Williams argues that four fundamental human needs are threatened when individuals or groups are unseen and unheard—belonging, self-esteem, control, and meaningful existence.

Though some may see these intangibles as non-necessities of life, they are truly needs. Williams explains that "'there is substantial evidence that when any of them are lacking,' people 'exhibit pathological consequences beyond mere temporal distress.'"[44] The four fundamental needs provide a crucial lens throughout this book to assess the presence of muteness and invisibility in African American young men.

Fundamental Human Need One: Belonging

Belonging may be the most fundamental human need. Studies have shown the need to belong is so important that without it, "people suffer mental and physical illness, and are rendered incapacitated."[45] For Williams, belonging requires consistent interactions in a temporarily stable environment with a few people who are concerned for one another's welfare. When one is *cut dead* or ostracized, affiliation and intimacy are imperiled, and even environments once deemed stable and enduring are perceived as precarious.[46] Williams explains how the silent treatment threatens feelings of belonging and hopes for affiliation, intimacy, and a stable environment much more than a heated argument. To demonstrate this, Williams compares a heated argument with the silent treatment:

> Both [the silent treatment and the heated argument] are clearly aversive, but, within the argument, there is an interaction. . . . The same cannot be said for being the target of the silent treatment. . . . There is no back-and-forth, no playing field on which to relate to others. For all intents and purposes, it is as though the target no longer exists.[47]

The connection is clear, then, between being seen and heard and a sense of belonging. Lacking back-and-forth conversation, eye contact, or other forms of recognition not only threatens a sense of belonging but also has the power to harm self-esteem.

Fundamental Human Need Two: Self-Esteem

"How do I feel others perceive my goodness and worth?" is a question resting at the core of self-esteem. Being *cut dead* adversely affects our self-esteem because going unrecognized and unheard sparks a negative internal dialogue that eats away at the target. According to Williams, this corrosive internal dialogue takes one of two forms. On one hand, the target may feel that he is being ostracized because he has done something wrong. Without the benefit of conversation or visible recognition from the source, the target generates a list of infractions that might warrant such unpleasant treatment. The growing list of plausible reasons for mistreatment threatens the target's own perception of his goodness and worth. On the other hand, the target may feel set apart and not acknowledged because of stigmas attached to deviance, physical appearance, or behaviors not fitting the norm. In this regard, the target not only questions his potential wrongdoing but also starts an internalized debate about whether he is desirable, wanted, or even capable of fitting in.

Williams also explains how the length of attacks on self-esteem affects the target. In the short run, resilient persons may draw upon defense mechanisms that affirm goodness or reflect on redeeming qualities tested during the attack. However, prolonged attacks on self-esteem can trigger defeatist thinking, prompt self-fulfilling prophecies, and ultimately create a downward spiral into lower self-esteem and undesirable behaviors.[48]

Fundamental Human Need Three: Control

"Why do I feel trapped?" one who is lacking control may ask. The belief that one has control and the capacity to change an undesirable situation gives one energy to persist in the face of failure.[49] However, when persons are *cut dead*, control is greatly diminished because with no substantive interaction with the source, the target has little capacity to alter his situation. Consider again the case of the teenager given the silent treatment for 153 days. The stance taken by her peers was unilateral as the group exerted its power over her. She was not seen. She was not heard. There was no give-and-take. One would imagine that she would have felt some sense of control even if they verbally berated her because, in spite of the negativity, the give-and-take of heated conversation would have at least provided her a sense of control.[50] Instead of participating in heated arguments and inflammatory remarks, this young woman was muted and made invisible, while her peers were seemingly unaffected. Not afforded the agency of give-and-take exchanges with her assailants, the teenager asserts the only measure of control she knows and attempts suicide. When that failed, and she was given the silent treatment a second time, she chose to mute herself. The loss of control over one's lot in life is evidenced in the stories of each of the young men chronicled in this book and is recognizable in the lives of countless young African American men who are *cut dead* on a daily basis.

Fundamental Human Need Four: Meaningful Existence

Without a sense of control, such young people may wonder, "What if I didn't exist?" Being cut dead, deliberately ignored, and completely snubbed evokes this deeply visceral, emotionally wrenching, existential question. Terror management theory argues that a fear of our own mortality and meaningless existence is a fundamental human anxiety that drives social behaviors.[51] If this is the case, persons who are muted and made invisible would be forced continuously to contemplate the fragility of their existence and ponder whether their lives have meaning and worth. The suicide attempt of the teenager given the silent treatment is evidence that she felt her life lacked meaning and that her peers viewed her presence as inconsequential. The unnamed protagonist in Ralph Ellison's *Invisible Man* most eloquently explains:

> You're constantly being bumped against by those of poor vision. Or again, you doubt if you really exist. You wonder whether you aren't simply a phantom in other people's minds. Say, a figure in a nightmare which the sleeper tries with all his strength to destroy. It's when you feel like that, out of resentment, you begin to bump people back. And let me admit, you feel that way most of the time. You ache with the need to convince yourself that you do exist in the real world, that you are a part of all the sound and anguish, and you strike out with your fists, you curse and you swear to make them recognize you. And, alas, it's seldom successful.[52]

The young men whose stories are recounted in this book fall along a wide spectrum of responses to being cut dead and having their self-worth challenged. While some plummet into depression and do harm to themselves, others lash out violently in disgust to gain visibility and voice.

Beyond Neediness: "Abundance Is Invisible"

A dear friend and community activist, De Amon "The Roving Listener" Harges, lives by the mantra "abundance is invisible." From this I gather that even in the absence of fundamental human needs, gifts and talents are present, but unnoticed. As Harges has found in his work, one must learn to see abundance, which is not as readily discernible as the more glaring need (or lack thereof). This search for gifts amidst absent fundamental human needs leads me to this question: how might abundance exist in the lives of the marginalized when control, self-esteem, meaningful existence, and belonging are in jeopardy?

To answer this question, one might examine the lives of biblical prophets and modern-day activists who found solace and home on the margins. It is not illogical that eccentric people that decry discomforting messages and characteristically upset the status quo, would lack belonging and understanding. Neither is it shocking that the resulting isolation would evoke internal attacks on self-esteem and the meaningfulness of existence. This book uncovers how these seemingly disempowering effects of being cut dead can be reframed into modicums of agency that inspire the muted and invisible to take back control over their lives. (The term *agency* means that an individual or community has volition and power to make independent choices.) This agency compels the young men and those caring for them to confront the negative internal banter with actions that build community and affirm self-worth.

Chapters 3 through 6 further explore these four fundamental human needs to illuminate specific areas threatened in the lives of young men who feel muted and invisible. The voids created by these threatened needs and the subsequent responses of the young men may be more detectable in some cases than in others because ostracism must be viewed temporally. According to Williams, short-term effects of ostracism may compel individuals (behaviorally, emotionally, and cognitively) to fight lost or threatened needs with the spiritual fervor of social dynamite.[53] However, prolonged exposure to continuous and repeated ostracism may lead to despair and helplessness; and like social junk, the cut dead may succumb because their needs have not been met.[54] Before examining how caregivers ensure that these four fundamental human needs are not threatened, contemplation on the caregiver's approach to caring with marginalized populations is imperative.

A Final Word: Invisible Assumptions

The meaning of our lives, and the memories of them, belong to the living, just as our funerals do.

—Thomas Lynch, *The Undertaking*

These grimly calming words from Thomas Lynch, an undertaker and the author of the award-winning book *The Undertaking: Life Studies of a Dismal Trade*, echo the words of a lesser-known funeral director by the name of Spencer Leaks. Unlike Lynch's decades of service in the sleepy suburban towns of Michigan, Leaks's years of service in the death industry were logged in the inner-city corridors of Chicago. In describing the urban terrain of his business, Leaks notes that over the last ten to fifteen years, 90 percent of the homicides he serviced were of African American young people.[55] More chilling, however, were Leaks's observations about role-playing at funerals: "[The young people] come to these funerals and I watch them, and they put themselves in the place of the person in the casket. The young people are in reality saying this is what I want to happen when I'm killed."[56] Lynch's and Leaks's logic lead another to conclude funerals serve as dress rehearsals for death. But far too many African American young men audition for their demise in the days of their youth. Guided by invisible assumptions that "at least in a casket they'll be viewed and seen," these young men cast themselves for tragic futures.

Passed over with no account given, cut-dead African American young men are trailed by the shadow of death from gang-infested city streets onto lush, green college campuses. By learning to see and hear more acutely, caregivers can penetrate the sphere of historic and present stereotypes, criminalizing stigmas, and invisible assumptions encircling the lives of African American young men. The framework of care introduced in the following pages furnishes caregivers with tools to bolster hope and to identify adaptive survival strategies to aid the strangely free African American young men who are cut dead but still alive.

w. e. b. darwin

In the fog &

In the night

there comes a sense

of second sight

the gift of gab to rouse the bear

and calm the mouse with gentle care

in the cave, i hibernate

& to the mouse hole i escape

in neither place do i find home

to lay my head

i am the lone

then to the treetops I retreat

unfurl my wings in nested seat

adaptation is the key

not second sight

but I have three.

—Gregory C. Ellison II

CHAPTER TWO

FROM GOLDEN DAYS TO IVY GREENS: CARING WITH MARGINALIZED POPULATIONS

For five Mondays in the heat of New Jersey's summer, I traveled forty-one miles north from the "quiet greenness"[1] of Princeton's campus into the white noise of Newark's brick city. The varied silences from south to north were deafening, maddening even. On these ninety-minute drives my mind raced like the speedometer, and "the wheel felt like an alien thing in my hands as I followed the white line of the highway. Heat rays from the late afternoon sun arose from the gray concrete"[2] and burned a solitary question into my own gray matter. How does it feel to be a ~~problem~~?[3]

W. E. B. Du Bois asked this of his readers (and himself) in the opening pages of *The Souls of Black Folk* (1903). One hundred and three years later, as a faculty member at the W. E. B. Du Bois Scholars Institute at Princeton University, I found this age-old question haunting me, driving me. Little did I know that the tensions of freedom and captivity implicated in this question would have a similar effect on the students enrolled in my seminar on identity development entitled "The Souls of Black Folk (Millennium Edition)." It was the third year I had taught the course at the summer institute, but this year was different. While seventy of America's brightest minority male and female high-school students gathered in the ivy-covered buildings of Princeton's campus for five weeks of intensive study in classes ranging from neuroscience to continental philosophy, I entered my classroom that first Monday morning in July and was greeted by twelve inquisitive African American young women. Every female student enrolled in the course appeared excited about the opportunity to study at Princeton, hopeful about the future, and eager to embark on a liberating journey of critical introspection. To be sure, I was inspirited by their presence and their eagerness to learn, but the class was not completely designed for young women. The physical lack of males was apparent.

By early evening my migration north began, but there was little freedom in the brick city, for on those five Mondays I was also slated to teach at Uth Turn, a nonprofit organization founded to teach life skills to young men coming out of prison. Once at my destination, I parked in a gated lot under video surveillance and walked to two locked brown metal doors. I pushed a button, leaned in, and spoke into the video-monitored call box. There, I identified myself as the Uth Turn on-site counselor. No response. A buzzer sounded that released the locks on the two brown metal doors. I proceeded up some stairs and approached the secretary, and she directed me to the classroom for my session. It was behind the *church* sanctuary. Around 6:15 p.m., on that first Monday evening in July, in the secured confines of God's house, I was greeted by twenty-two despairing African American young men who were frustrated about their present circumstances, reluctant to think of what the future might hold, and openly resistant to any introspective work. The internal void was apparent.

Hours later, nightfall approaches. I reenter my car, overwhelmed, over-loaded. As I pull out of the secured facility, I notice the sun of **"the Golden Day"** nestling into the horizon behind me, and now not only does the wheel feel alien, but so do I.[4]

For the next four Mondays that July, I relived the same sequence: morning classes in the open, lush greenness of Princeton's campus clashing against evening sessions of restraint and confined gloom in the brick city. The varied silences from south to north were deafening, maddening even. On each of those Mondays, as **the Golden Day** vanished into eventide, three questions flooded into my consciousness. How do I care with authenticity? Who's on whose margins? Where do I position myself to serve?

In spite of the endless internal chatter, the silence in the car is deafening. The gleam of my headlights pierces the darkness. I follow the white lines of the highway, and my questions ultimately end where they began: how does it feel to be a ~~problem~~?

The shift from suburban campus to city streets symbolically marks the daily travels of many persons challenged to care while moving between seemingly disparate worlds. Entering into these spaces, the caregiver may be tasked to minister to persons relegated to the margins and to choose the appropriate approach to care. The task of caring is further complicated if the caregiver also finds herself feeling marginalized. The alienlike sensation of moving between worlds, caring for the cut dead, and reckoning with one's own sense of marginality grounds this chapter. This chapter is subdivided into four sections that focus intently and separately on the four words *caring with marginalized populations*. These subsections outline four approaches to care, the fluidity of marginality, issues of critical distance, and the caregiver's wholeness, respectively. Examination of the word *with* concludes the chapter to accentuate the mutual benefits of care experienced between the marginalized and the caregiver.

Caring: Four Approaches

In *Images of Pastoral Care: Classic Readings*, Robert Dykstra charts the long history of pastoral theologians who use metaphorical images as guiding frameworks for theoretical analysis and therapeutic practice.[5] In his text, Dykstra highlights nineteen different images that have shaped pastoral theological theory and practice (e.g., Seward Hiltner's solicitous shepherd, Edward Wimberly's indigenous storyteller, and Brita Gill-Austern's reticent outlaw). In 2010, in an article entitled "From My Center to the Center of All Things," I joined the ranks of image-conscious pastoral theologians and proposed the metaphor of the hourglass to guide caring practices.[6]

Although metaphors prove useful in tracing the history of pastoral care and in moving students from theory to practice, in my experience they fail to connect these same students with the gut-wrenching visceral realities associated with caring. In an effort to pull on the heartstrings of students enrolled in my elective "Caring for Marginalized Populations," I moved away from the classic metaphors. Instead, I introduced these students to four passages in pastoral theological and popular literature that communicate the weight, urgency, and introspection caregivers face as they move into unfamiliar spaces, walk alongside the *cut dead*, and traverse disparate worlds.

Care as Radical Presence

Extracted from Henri Nouwen's *Out of Solitude*, the first passage presents the caregiver as fully present even in voided spaces. Nouwen, a Catholic priest, prolific writer, and professor who dedicated his life to mining the interior, advocating peace, and standing in solidarity with the poor in spirit, spoke of care in this way:

> The word *care* finds it roots in the Gothic "Kara," which means "lament." The basic meaning of care is to grieve, to experience sorrow, to cry out with. I am very much struck by this background of the word *care* because we tend to look at caring as an attitude of the strong toward the weak, of the powerful toward the powerless, of the haves toward the have-nots. And, in fact, we feel quite uncomfortable with an invitation to enter into someone's pain before doing something with it . . . [Instead] the friend who can be silent with us in a moment of despair and confusion, who can stay with us in an hour of grief and bereavement, who can tolerate not-knowing, not curing, not healing and face with us the reality of our powerlessness, this is the friend who cares . . .
>
> Therefore, to care means first of all to be present to each other. From experience you know that those who care for you become present to you. When they listen, they listen to you. When they speak, you know they speak to you. And when they ask questions, you know it is for your sake and not for their own. Their presence is a healing presence because they accept you on your terms and they encourage you to take your own life seriously.[7]

In discussion of this passage, students struck by Nouwen's humility testify to the steadfast resolve of a caregiver unmoved by stilled silence, tolerant of not knowing divine will, and steadied even in the powerlessness of the human condition. Student consensus often characterizes this approach as one of radical presence. However, many students enrolled in the "Caring for Marginalized Populations" class enter Candler with vocational interests in social justice ministry. These activist-minded students find that Nouwen's approach alone is anemic, for care that does not advocate for the voiceless is shorthanded.

Care as Passionate Advocacy

To complement Nouwen's radical presence, I introduce Pearl Cleage's personal manifesto, "Why I Write" Cleage, an award-winning playwright, accomplished novelist, and African American womanist, articulates the unyielding pressure she feels to write as a form of advocacy for those robbed of voice and visibility. Her manifesto narrates the unending cycle of violence inflicted upon her female students, friends, and relatives. She even recounts her own undergraduate experience during which her boyfriend bound her hands and feet and told her, "If [he] couldn't have [her], nobody could."[8] From this space of existential angst and internal pain, Cleage pens her diatribe against violence and lists the reasons why she writes:

> I am writing because five women a day are murdered by the men who say they love them. I am writing because rape is. I am writing because I am a daughter and a mother and a lover and a sister and a womanist. . . . I am writing because I have seen my sisters tortured and tormented by the fathers of their children. I am writing because I almost married a man who beat me regularly with no remorse. I am writing because my daughter is almost old enough to start "dating" and I don't know how to tell her to protect herself from what I cannot even fully articulate myself.
>
> I am writing to allow myself to feel the anger. I am writing to keep from running toward it or away from it or into anybody's arms. I am writing to find solutions and pass them on. I am writing to find a language and pass it on.
>
> I am writing, writing, writing, for my life.[9]

In considering Cleage's words as an approach to care, I ask each student to read aloud one sentence from the above paragraph. As the diverse voices fill the room, students are challenged to imaginatively substitute the word *care* every time Cleage uses the word *write*. In seconds, Cleage's torrent of advocacy against violence floods the room, and students bear the weight of urgency and abiding commitment associated with caring. Without fail, every class sits in silence after Cleage's final word. When the quiet is broken, students characterize this approach to care as a passionate advocacy marked by sacrifice, courage, and commitment. The question then emerges, how does one care passionately when the person or community seeking care feels too broken to have anything to offer and stands in suspicion of the caregiver's benevolent intentions?

Care as Authentic Connection

Well-intentioned seminary students armed with psychological theories and theological training still frequently inquire how they can relate to people of different ethnicity, socioeconomic class, and cultural background. To these queries, my left brain is tempted to unfold a critical exposé of Emmanuel Lartey's intercultural theory, "we are like all others, we are like some others, and we are like no others."[10] However, recognizing that these students are searching for answers extending beyond theory, my right brain opts to introduce to them a poem by accomplished writer and scholar Mari Evans entitled "Celebration," which says when we each bring a whole person "we will have us twice as much / of love and everything." The poem talks about bringing together battered hearts that must be treated gently. Even though we bring our imperfect selves, the unity makes twice as much as we have by ourselves.

Evans's poem genuinely celebrates the imperfect yet storied life of a caregiver who brings a whole heart and lays it down carefully before another. Likewise, she celebrates the courage and hopefulness of the one seeking care who brings a story with all its own chips and rust. Not only does Evans's model of a genuine presentation of one heart to another stand against traditional caring practices of the haves to the have-nots, but also it fully appreciates the storied life and wisdom of the person seeking care. It sees the one before the caregiver as whole, as human, and as made in the image of God; not as a statistic, a case number, or another needy parishioner to check off the list. Students laud and fear Evans's authentic sharing because caring authentically requires unabashed self-reckoning with one's own story.

A recurring theme present in every case throughout this book shows that the cut dead can smell inauthenticity from a mile away. In light of suspicions and potential stigmas related to their position, caregivers garner rapport by valuing the stories of others, while not undermining the inherent wisdom in their own story. While the caregiver's complete and full disclosure is likely misguided, unwarranted, and unwise, an introspective look at one's life history is a resource for care. As will be discussed in chapter 4, caregivers who can strategically present their own story in a modestly confrontational way have the potential to awaken dormant hopes in the cut dead and in themselves, leading both parties to be twice as strong and true. However, caregivers unwilling to authentically mine their inner resources, while expecting the cut dead to do interior work, are hypocritical and risk being discovered as fraud.

Such a strong supposition for authenticity alarms students equipped only with good intentions and theoretical knowledge. Reality sinks in that present, passionate, authentic care involves significant risks.

Care as Perspectival

Recognizing the risks of being fully present in the seat of trauma, standing stalwart as an advocate in the face of oppression, and offering one's whole self in order to receive the fullness of the other seems all-consuming and overwhelming to the most well-intentioned student. These demanding tasks of the caregiver are coupled with the accompanying stressors of moving into unfamiliar spaces and interacting with unfamiliar people. By this point in the class, discussion of approaches to care, students have knotted stomachs and wonder aloud how such a caregiver remains sane. To these cries for caregiving solace, I offer selections from Bonnie J. Miller-McLemore's article "Contemplation in the Midst of Chaos: Contesting the Maceration of the Theological Teacher."[12]

While targeted primarily to an audience of theological teachers, this article has served as a useful tool in easing the anxieties of prospective caregivers feeling inundated with the unforeseen stresses of caring. In her article, Miller-McLemore references the "cacophony of demands" that increases failure and chops the minister's focus, time, vision, vocation, and contemplative acreage into small pieces.[13]

As an antidote to ministerial maceration, she offers a perspectival change. The shift in perspective is encouraged through a nuanced examination of the article's title. In short, she warns caregivers not to contemplate (or to fix one's attention) *on* chaos, because focus on surrounding chaos macerates hope and seeds despair. Instead, she challenges caregivers to alter their vantage point and see the redemptive role of chaos where spirituality appears out of disruption, interruption, and confusion. This altered line of sight allows the caregiver to sit in stilled silence when no verbal answer suffices. It ennobles the caregiver to crusade against oppressive forces when those seeking care have little power to stand. It drives the caregiver to fully share his story and hear and see the story of the cut dead when others believe the cut dead have nothing to offer. Contemplation *in the midst of* chaos, and not *on* the chaos, is a sanctifying perspective that sees God's creative work in disorder and disarray.

Marginalized: Assessing the Margins and the Shifting Center

Though this book focuses primarily on African American young men who are unseen and unheard, in the introduction the case is made that the unacknowledged are all around us and the cut dead are hidden before us in plain view. This notion may prove problematic for some as it troubles the convenient binaries of "us and them," "haves and have-nots." I often pose the following question to students: how would their perspectives of care alter if they came to see that in certain instances the *us's* and *haves* were the marginalized and the *thems* and *have-nots* wielded power from the center?

In an article entitled "Who's on Whose Margins?" Australian health sciences scholar Michael Hurley troubles the notion of marginalization as a static reality and problematizes the view that marginalized persons lack power. On one hand, marginality structures social differences between groups; marks economic, cultural, and political differences; and "organizes these differences in relation to unequal distribution of power."[14] However, on the other hand, Hurley believes conceptualizing marginality in this way is far too simple. He unfolds the idea that the metaphor of margins is evasive:

> Is this a spatial metaphor? Are we dealing here with a page (the margins) or a circle (the centre)? Is the metaphor geographical (city as rich centre, regions as poor thus peripheral)? Is the metaphor more abstractly conceived as a power relation (powerful/powerless) and then applied economically or socially (centre/periphery)? If so, how do we deal with changes over time?[15]

The final question in the block quote regarding change identifies Hurley's central supposition that margin and center are dynamic forces that constantly shift. In this regard, those deemed on the margin are not always everywhere marginal, and power, while unevenly distributed, does not always rest in the hands of the haves, who are most often at the center. History demonstrates that groups categorically deemed as marginal and powerless have been catalysts in combating racism, colonialism, and sexism. The margin becomes the centerpiece of change.

Although this book highlights young men at both ends of the socioeconomic spectrum who are victims of ostracism, it does not seek to valorize the category of African American young men who are cut dead as marginal. Instead, it seeks to highlight new possibilities for caregivers and African American young men to envision power shifts from center to margin. In so doing, I hope that the proposals hereafter will catalyze African American young men who feel unacknowledged, and those who care about them, to seize the inherent power that historically has originated on the margins and forced change throughout the annals of time.

The Golden Day Revisited: Margins on Center Stage

In light of the transformational power existent on the margins and the necessity for caregivers to shatter the simple binaries that mark *who's on whose margins*, recall the first pages of this chapter and the capitalized and emboldened phrase, **the Golden Day**. The accentuation of this phrase is, indeed, intentional. In *Invisible Man*, the Golden Day is a rowdy bar on the outskirts of town that also functions as a bordello and place of respite for institutionalized war veterans. At first glance, the Golden Day serves as a spatial metaphor—a marginal gathering place for marginal people. The raucous bar and brothel stand in stark contrast to the more centrally located college campus and its refined students described in previous chapters of the novel. A closer look reveals striking similarities between these seemingly contrasting worlds and among the persons who walk their grounds. It further proves that for caregivers like me, who move from campus green to city streets, marginality lies in the eye of the beholder.

Upon entering the Golden Day, the unnamed protagonist describes a world that, at first sight, is just a rowdy bar. Packing the barroom are institutionalized African American war veterans who, prior to the shell shock of war, held positions of prominence as doctors, lawyers, and teachers. Interestingly, Ralph Ellison does not refer to these once hopeful, now institutionalized veterans as "patients," but instead he labels them as "chain gang members" and "inmates." This label is not a mistake but is emblematic of African American men who are imprisoned by psychological wounds and who are at war with marginalizing social forces that deem them as an explosive threat to society or a discardable commodity. Regardless of their gifts or buried hopes, both the disabled veterans at the Golden Day and the individuals I counseled at Uth Turn in Newark were viewed askance, if viewed at all.

Ralph Ellison also charts the evolution of how the building, currently housing the Golden Day, had been used over the years: "It was a church, then a bank, then it was a restaurant and a fancy gambling house, and now we got it. . . . I think somebody said it used to be a jailhouse, too."[16] One should not overlook the psychological impress of structures that confine people in the name of safety. The heavy surveillance of the church housing Uth Turn had numerous structural similarities to the prison facilities in which the young men were living. Secured within the confines of God's house, the stigmatized and psychologically wounded "inmates" of Uth Turn harden their exterior to guard their inner core, as they did while incarcerated. It is also not surprising that under these psychological and structural conditions chaos would occasionally emerge.

In contrast to the Golden Day and its rowdy inmates, Ralph Ellison casts the lush, green college campus as a place of tranquility and peace, filled with straightlaced, ambitious students. More detailed observation reveals that the students, like those at the Golden Day, also bear psychological wounds and struggle with issues of identity. The unnamed protagonist, also an invisible man, is one of these, a talented collegian and the model of this internal struggle. The commonality of woundedness found in the criminalized inmate and the idealized student reveals that marginalized people cannot be spatially pinpointed with accuracy. Curiously, the inmates in the Golden Day and the unnamed protagonist, at different points in the novel, resist their labels and revolt, suggesting that even those deemed marginal can harness internal powers and enact change.

Finally, *Invisible Man* speaks particularly to this book's topic because the unnamed protagonist bears not only the role of a student but also that of a caregiver, commissioned as a driver for a wealthy trustee visiting the college's campus. While giving the trustee a tour through surrounding towns, the protagonist is compelled by an unforeseen and tragic turn of events to drive from the serenity of the campus into the chaos of the Golden Day. At the Golden Day, an inner conflict ensues for the protagonist, and he is forced to make difficult decisions regarding his own safety and that of the trustee under his care. Like many caregivers, he finds himself making reasoned choices as he moves nimbly between the disparate worlds of the Golden Day and the campus. He must broker such questions as: How and where should I offer care? Who are my allies? What are the consequences of my actions, and when is it safe to proceed? To make the protagonist's situation even more complex, he remains invisible. We, as caregivers, face similar challenges, as we move between margin and center, confront our own internal disarray, and engage different populations.

Populations: Research Methods as Social Action

While *population* is a widely accepted term in social research, this designation may present problems for caregivers seeking to passionately and authentically care for *persons* relegated to the margins. In its strictest, most traditional sense, social research governed by scientific objectivity views persons (or populations) as "objects" to be studied. Furthermore, this objective (or post-positivist) research paradigm casts the inquirer in the role of an "expert" who has special, perhaps unmerited, insight about the populations being studied. To derive knowledge, this expert carefully observes and measures what happens "out there" in the population.[17] In sum, the researcher is the bearer of all knowledge, while the "population" is held at bay as little more than potential data.

For some, this characterization of objective research may not sound troubling, but for others, relegating persons who are already stigmatized, marginalized, and cut dead to "object" status remains unacceptable practice. In contrast to the objectivist approach, action research is an advocacy-oriented methodology that realigns hierarchy by seeing populations as "subjects" who are experts of their own story. As experts, the "subjects" collaborate with the inquiring researcher, and as a team, the inquirer and subject "cogenerate relevant knowledge" to create a more satisfying outcome for all stakeholders involved.[18]

Viewing "populations" as experts who collaborate in creating relevant knowledge and working from theory to practice are principles familiar to practical theologians; a principle, according to John Swinton and Harriet Mowat, that is much more than seeing the world differently. For Swinton and Mowat:

> The primary task of Practical Theology is not simply to see differently, but to enable that revised vision to create changes in the way that Christians and Christian communities perform the faith. Practical Theology is certainly a reflective discipline, but above all else, it is a theology of action.[19]

Rather than viewing persons being researched as objects or sterile populations that are "over there" or somehow foreign, I advocate a practical theological frame of action research as a preferred methodology and guiding principle for service with the cut dead. Such service *with* and among this "population" involves heightened awareness and constant, sometimes subversive, negotiation.

With: Embracing the Problem Status of Liminality

Seldom do we include the words *subversive* and *pastor* in the same sentence. Largely because in modern contexts, "to subvert" generally carries a negative connotation and is usually equated with overthrowing, upsetting, or overturning an institution—for example, a government or religion—from its foundation. It is not difficult to conceptualize community activists or prophetic ministers (such as Gandhi, Dr. Martin Luther King, Jr., Malcolm X, or Nelson Mandela) as subversive agents, who negotiate relationships and use understandings of communal dynamics to upset the body politic and to lead the marginalized to more just circumstances. However, it may not be as easy to imagine pastoral caregivers in this revolutionary role.

Pastoral caregivers are pastors, chaplains, or counselors who inspire and instruct congregations, students, patients, clients, and even other pastors on how to better care for themselves and other souls in need. They are intellectual practitioners whose caring acts are rarely seen as overthrowing, overturning, or upsetting people or institutions. But I propose that pastoral caregivers can, and indeed do, act subversively, though typically in a less obtrusive way than a fiery revolutionary acts.

Pastoral caregivers carefully navigate relationships *with* individuals from vastly different worlds in order to be of service to diverse communities. In some respects, pastoral caregivers are professionals without a home. In the academy, while possessing the intellectual acumen to "rouse the bear" of colleagues, because their attention to practice stands counter to the modern research university's emphasis on specialization and scientific objectivity, pastoral caregivers have long operated on the margins of the academy. Some of their academic peers have questioned the rigor, merit, and sophistication of their scholarship. At the same time, pastoral caregivers—many of whom are intuitively gifted and specially trained to enter the mouse holes of trauma—may find it difficult to call the church their home. Though often ordained ministers, many pastoral caregivers may not themselves serve as a pastor of a church. Living on the borders of these institutions gives them insight into the marginality of persons, communities, and issues that are discarded and overlooked by other disciplines and professionals.

While situated in "in-but-not-of" circumstances, the pastoral caregiver is equipped with academic and therapeutic analytical techniques and is expected to process the stories of diverse people from diverse backgrounds and reorient them to a more hopeful outlook. She must be savvy enough to navigate the politics and relationships of being in, but not of, academic, ecclesial, armed forces, or any number of other communities. Responsible for uncovering and extracting common themes in diverse stories, the pastoral caregiver stands as a bridge between the community and the church, psychology and theology, theory and practice, and, sometimes, suburban and urban. Thus, to effect individual or communal change, each of these radical tasks must be subversively performed under the mild-mannered, oft-questioned moniker of pastoral caregiving.

To serve effectively as a bridge between diverse disciplines and divergent communities, the pastoral caregiver as subversive agent must be conscious of critical distance. For the purposes of this chapter, *critical distance* refers to the social, cultural, ideological, or behavioral differences between individuals or communities. Though the liminal status of pastoral caregivers helps them identify with some of this cut-dead population of young men, keeping a sense of critical distance is vital to their work.

To address how caregivers have chosen to stand *with* marginalized populations and not just relegate them to being "objects" of study, there are three exemplary primary theorists who have written and lectured extensively on their engagement with and advocacy for various communities. The late Edward Said, once an accomplished pianist and holder of an endowed chair in English and comparative literature at Columbia University, was exiled from his homeland of Palestine at the age of twelve and subsequently approached his intellectual work as an outsider commissioned to speak truth to power.[20] Michael Walzer, a Jewish intellectual, worked on collaborative projects related to the history of Jewish political thought and was much more guarded about his personal history. Emphasizing more of a communal sensibility, Walzer, an emeritus faculty member of Princeton University's Institute for Advanced Study, contends that the intellectual is vastly weakened in isolation; hence, the cultural critic must be invariably connected to community. W. E. B. Du Bois occupies a liminal space that is representative of countless figures in the African American intellectual tradition. He is arguably the most towering African American intellectual of the twentieth century and was the first black recipient of a doctorate from Harvard University. Though these theorists do not directly address the discipline of pastoral care, their varied approaches to critical distance exemplify the role of subversive activity in the academy and offer a fresh perspective on how pastoral caregivers may carve out space for analysis of individuals, communities, and self.

A Voice from the Wilderness: Said's Internal Critic

Based on his 1993 Reith Lectures, later published as *Representations of the Intellectual*, Edward Said argues that in order to be critical of the oppressor and the oppressed group for which one advocates, the intellectual must *step back* as a detached observer. Said outlines the public role of the intellectual as serving neither as a pacifier nor as a consensus-builder, but instead working from a place of exile, as one who speaks truth to power and disturbs the status quo.[21] The exiled intellectual is constantly at odds with systems of power, so Said argues for the intellectual to detach from community to lessen the risk of being co-opted by governments and corporations. From this vantage point, as an outsider looking in, the exiled intellectual not only "raise[s] embarrassing questions to confront orthodoxy and dogma" but also sees the challenges facing the oppressed as interrelated. When detached, the exiled intellectual has the wide scope of seeing "things both in terms of what has been left behind and what is actual in the here and now," while also seeing "things not as they are but as they have come to be that way."[22] Here, from the fringes, the exiled intellectual advocates for people on the margins and calls for universal human principles and basic standards of freedom and justice from worldly powers to be upheld.[23]

For the subversive caregiver seeking to fight for the needs of the unac-knowledged, the communal detachment of Said's exiled position evokes some questions. Are such intellectuals forced out of community, I wonder, or do they choose to become outsiders? If the latter, does not chosen exile then suggest a prior sense of professional privilege and personal power—a power that is rarely afforded African American persons seeking to bring truth to light?[24] Furthermore, we might ask if separation from the people whom one is seeking to help compromises the credibility of one's work. It strikes me that the weak and underrepresented may find it difficult to make connections between their own daily struggles and the lived reality of intellectuals who, for all the empowering thought in their written work, remain sequestered in the ivory tower and seemingly out of reach.

Inches from the Struggle: Walzer's Connected Intellectual

Michael Walzer suggests that removal from the public sphere is crucially disadvantageous to the social critic. Instead, he advocates for an intellectual who measures critical distance in inches.[25] In his Tanner Lectures at Harvard University in 1985, which were later compiled into *Interpretation and Social Criticism,* Walzer deconstructs the conventional view of the detached observer and redefines an alternative perspective of the intellectual. As a connected critic, the intellectual serves as a "local judge" who garners his or her authority, or the lack thereof, by engaging in communal protest with the disenfranchised. Seeing little value in being intellectually or emotionally detached, Walzer characterizes this critic as "one of us," an intellectual who appeals to "local or localized principles."[26] Thus, he advocates for a cultural critic who *steps into* "the thicket of moral experience where they are intimately known," not a detached intellectual who *steps back* from parochial concerns.[27]

There is great utility in the approach of the connected critic, with which some pastoral caregivers working alongside the underrepresented might readily identify; however, how does the connected critic, who lodges herself in the "thicket of moral experience," create the space needed to critically analyze the community or individual of interest and the powers over them? Walzer contends that the intellectual becomes a critic "by elaborating on existing moralities and telling stories about a society more just than, though not entirely different from, our own."[28] Here Walzer's connected critic implicitly creates critical distance to engage in reflective work in the midst of praxis and immersion in the storied lives of community.

Although praxis indeed inspires and enlivens intellectual work, the cultural critic who follows this model risks becoming an "unsuccessful intellectual" whose parochial sensibilities limit his prophetic voice. As an example, the Reverend Al Sharpton was the first of the 2004 presidential candidates to address the issue of gay marriage. However, heterosexual and homosexual persons alike largely dismissed him because in being deemed so pro-black, he was also perceived as possibly anti-white. But neither the critical distance created by the physical space of Said's more detached critic nor the praxis-oriented reflective space of Walzer's connected critic fully encapsulate the space needed for the subversive caregiver to thrive or to address African American young men who are unseen and unheard. For that, we must turn again to an icon in the African American intellectual tradition: W. E. B. Du Bois.

Inner Landscape as Tool of Resistance: Du Bois and Internal Intellectuals

To the real question, how does it feel to be a problem? I answer seldom a word. And yet, being a problem is a strange experience—peculiar even for one who has never been anything else, save perhaps in boyhood and Europe.

—W. E. B. Du Bois, *The Souls of Black Folk*[29]

W. E. B. Du Bois (1868–1963), like many African American intellectuals, lived a marginal existence. To his dismay, Du Bois found that he was not only a problem to white America but also a foreigner in the black community, which he longed to call home. Du Bois's experience of double exile from black and white America represents a dilemma for countless African American intellectuals seeking a comfortable space to pursue their scholarship. Cornel West writes about the paradox of marginality and intellectual homelessness faced by "successful" and "unsuccessful" black intellectuals. He states:

> The "successful" black intellectual capitulates, often uncritically, to the prevailing paradigms and research programs of the white bourgeois academy, and the "unsuccessful" black intellectual remains encapsulated within the parochial discourses of Afro-American intellectual life.[30]

Within this reality, the African American intellectual is situated in a double bind because "the black community views both alternatives with distrust and disdain."[31] Additionally, there is no assurance that the "successful" intellectual will have her work taken seriously by peers in the white bourgeois academy.

History has shown that many African American intellectuals have been faced with the challenge of negotiating personal relationships and communal politics to aid those in need. Not possessing the privilege or power to completely remove themselves from their subjects of analysis, and unwilling to risk the delegitimizing label of being too parochially connected, some African American cultural critics have chosen to create critical distance by becoming first and foremost critical of self. By carving out this space in the mind, these internal critics seek to understand their own identity in relation to a larger system. Unremoved from the community, but cognizant of not being fully in it, this critic internalizes the pain of those around her. Truth to power is spoken, but from a place of shared humanity.

In her article "Black Women Intellectuals," bell hooks speaks of how this identity-shaping internal space influenced her own intellectual development:

> I became my own "enlightened witness," able to analyze the forces that were acting upon me, and through that understanding able to sustain a separate sense of my self. Wounded, at times persecuted and abused, I found the life of the mind a refuge, a sanctuary where I could experience a sense of agency and thereby construct my own subject identity.[32]

With a heightened awareness of the constructive and destructive forces impinging on one's self within the system, the African American intellectual is given a unique perspective to view how others in similar systems are affected. Cornel West also alludes to how this critical introspection can sharpen one's social analysis:

> Critical space and insurgent activity can be expanded. This expansion will occur more readily when Black intellectuals take a more candid look at themselves, the historical and social forces that shape them and the limited though significant resources of the community from whence they come. A critical "self-inventory" . . . that scrutinizes the social positions, class positions and cultural socializations of black intellectuals is imperative.[33]

Such a critical self-inventory is imperative for the pastoral theologian who functions subversively.

Unable to remove themselves completely from the system, pastoral theologians (regardless of ethnicity) must be sensitive to the guidance of their inner compass and must strategically determine, in the academy, church, and counseling environment, which issues can be broached without risking further marginalization for themselves or injury to those whom they seek to help. Given that this task of introspection is not an easy one, the African American intellectual and pastoral theologian is given respite in examining self and others through a "gift" that enables him to analyze and critique contrasting worlds.

W. E. B. Du Bois believed that African Americans who live liminally and navigate between divergent worlds are gifted with "second sight." Du Bois's biographer, David Levering Lewis, interprets this gift as an intuitive faculty of seeing and saying things about society with heightened moral validity because one understands the mind and heart of his oppressor, while experiencing existentially the pain and heartache of the oppressed.[34] This creative gift is possible for many African American intellectuals and bridge-building pastoral theologians of *all* racial and ethnic backgrounds who live an "in-but-not-of" existence. It cannot be overstated that the intuitive gift of second sight and its ability to aid in bolstering the hope of muted and invisible young men is accessible to *all* pastoral theologians and professionals who work within liminal spaces. That is to say, it is possible for people of all racial and ethnic backgrounds to reach out to young African American men who feel unseen and unheard, if they are willing to think and act as an internal critic. Failure to do so will lead to hopelessly ineffective interventions with these youth.

Pastoral caregivers have a unique role to subversively and strategically stand as a bridge between disparate worlds. Their intuitive faculty to see, understand, and feel the pain of the marginalized and those who marginalize them enables these caregivers to address the tensions within institutions such as the church and the academy and the dissonance between psychology and religion. This "bridging" for pastoral theologians may entail using ordinary objects (i.e., music, literature, or film) to convey hopeful meanings. It may involve subversively taking information from one source, encoding the language, and retransmitting it in another language to offer messages of hope. For instance, in working with populations in which counseling is stigmatized, to be of assistance to individuals in need, it may be necessary for the pastoral theologian to disguise her therapeutic techniques through mediums such as Bible studies, prayer meetings, or workshops. Often such indirect approaches are necessary in working with African American young men who experience muteness and invisibility and may be reluctant to engage in introspection.

A Final Word: w.e.b. darwin

In his studies on evolution, Charles Darwin found that all species evolve to survive. So too must caregivers—who move between seemingly disparate worlds to care with marginalized populations—adapt to changing people and terrain. Three such adaptations have been outlined. The exile, standing on the outer regions, peers from afar and speaks truth to power. The connected critic, entrenched in the thicket of struggle, finds herself inches away from subjects of concern. The internal critic, unable to retreat to exile or immerse in the thicket, finds wisdom within. In spite of radical presence, passionate advocacy, and subversive commitments, in order to communicate messages from center to margin and margin to center, these caregivers find themselves straddling both terrains. They are "in but not of" communities and don many faces to care. But in this straddling comes evolution and the emergence of second (or third) sight to see Golden Days in the dark nights of rage and to hear the cries of the cut dead but still alive.

WildKingdom

You say pay the price, but it's my life!

If it's a calculated risk, why am I holdin' dice?

This is the distinction between bears and mice

They're both in the wild, leading different lives

Now that I've gained hope, will I lose my
mind?

—William K. Gravely

CHAPTER THREE

THE DEATH OF CONTROL AND THE BIRTH OF FEARLESS DIALOGUE

The room erupted and the heated exchange further marked our differences. Voices competed for attention, yet no one was heard. Minutes earlier an even-tempered group discussion on vocational discernment quickly morphed into a firestorm of debate. In the verbal sparring, two Uth Turn mentors scalded Nathaniel for his choice to continue selling drugs upon his release. Above the fever pitch of voices he fired back, "You don't know me!" In smoldering rage he revealed the rationale behind his seemingly "errant" future plans. Then there was silence. His words singed the hearts of the rebuking mentors and sparked me to examine how caregivers might more effectively communicate with those who feel muted and cut dead.

Nathaniel's outburst surprised me because I had known him as one of the more respectful and levelheaded young men in the group. When we first met, he was nearly eighteen, convicted of drug possession with intent to sell, and aware that any future legal infractions would eliminate any possibility of him being treated as a minor. Prior to the aforementioned evening, Nathaniel and I had completed three individual "goal orientation" sessions[1] to identify the strengths and weaknesses of his support network and to begin framing his future plans beyond the program. In those sessions, he came across as mild-mannered and thoughtful, but any mention of his family triggered an unspoken rage, followed by uneasy silences.

Navigating delicately around his family of origin, we talked about his childhood, his struggles in school, and his challenges of moving beyond the label of "troublemaker." In our third session, on New Year's Eve, Nathaniel made passing comments about his willingness to change his attitude and work harder in the coming year, but he continually referenced his challenges with "keeping faith." When asked to say what he meant by "keeping faith," he explained, "If I'm at school and working up to my ability and nobody sees it, I get in trouble. They already think I'm bad. If I'm doing the best I can and nobody recognizes it, I might as well be bad. I guess I lose faith easy." After a few minutes of questioning about how he might not be so easily discouraged, Nathaniel mentioned a sermon that he recently heard. Unaware that I was an ordained Baptist minister, Nathaniel offered a colorful paraphrasing of John 21 and "the fisherman who couldn't catch fish."

Recounting the sermon, Nathaniel described that after a long day out on the water, the fisherman returned to shore with an empty net and no fish. The next morning the fisherman returned, and a man on the shore told him to throw the net on the other side of the boat. Imagining himself in the role of the fisherman, Nathaniel blurted out, "I'm thinking, I'm not gonna do it. But the fisherman didn't lose faith and catches more fish than his net can hold. The fisherman is a better man than me. I would have left instead of trying again. I wouldn't have thrown the net on the other side." For the next several minutes Nathaniel and I openly and honestly explored how he and the fisherman were "in the same boat," wrestling with faith, examining the suspiciousness of well-intentioned shore-side onlookers (like me), and considering the merits of trying something different to yield more favorable results. Little did I know that days later this conversation about keeping faith and future choices would be reignited in a more incendiary form when two unwitting mentors would push Nathaniel's trigger and prompt him to discharge the rage that he had held in for so long.

On that fateful evening, cornered and virtually unheard by the mentors, Nathaniel sat disquieted. His furrowed brow signaled the silence before the storm. Then suddenly, Nathaniel lashed back at the accusing mentors: "You don't know me! My mom's a crackhead. I got two younger sisters. My mom used to prostitute out of our house to get money for crack. I started selling drugs to my mom to protect my sisters from the men coming in our house." Silence fell upon the room. Mentors and Uth Turn participants alike contemplated the gravity of Nathaniel's words and the choice he made to slowly kill his mother to protect his sisters.

Nathaniel's life spiraled out of control long before he exploded on the deprecating mentors. Given his reflections on John 21, I gathered that at some point in his life Nathaniel was a faithful person. In good faith, he likely placed *control* of his best interests into the hands of others, who should have been well-meaning. At some point, he had faith in teachers. But in spite of his efforts to excel, he was only seen as a troublemaker. He had had faith in mentors, too, but their wisdom took precedence over hearing his story. In their eyes, he was no more than a hard-hearted drug dealer. Nathaniel even once had faith in his mother, but her addiction took priority over the safety of her children. Frustrated by the negligence of seemingly well-intentioned persons, Nathaniel could no longer keep faith in God.

Nathaniel could not control the perceptions of those who failed to hear his story and see him as more than a troublemaker and drug dealer. He found himself cornered by his mother's decision to bring strange men in contact with his young sisters. The ground of Nathaniel's faith in the world around him was crumbling beneath his feet. So, behind the strain of a furrowed brow, he seized control of the one thing he believed could gain him visibility and voice—his story.

Nathaniel's faithful step of authentic sharing initiated what I have come to call "fearless dialogue,"[2] a form of conversation marked by *shared control,* mutual vulnerability, and navigation through the potential pitfalls of narrative, space, and time. Drawing from tools in biblical and cultural studies, this chapter identifies three parameters of fearless dialogue: shared context of meaning, multivalent interpretation, and time-bending (also referred to as "reframing"). These parameters contest three paradoxes that diminish the potential development of fearless dialogue and threaten the fundamental human need of control.

Loss of Control and the Paradoxical Potholes That Stifle Conversation

Writing with the candor of a seasoned journalist, John Rich, who is also a physician and professor, pinpoints the visceral reactions shared by many after hearing newscasts involving violence and African American young men. In his recent book, *Wrong Place, Wrong Time,* Rich says:

Each time a shooting or a stabbing or an assault is reported in the news, the details obscure a young man with a story, a young man with real blood running through his veins. Without any access to their voices, we could easily formulate solutions that are out of sync with the realities of their lives and that would be ineffective or outright destructive. Without hearing their stories we lose sight of these young men who hold real hope for the future, whose visions for community embrace peace and nonviolence. This is why hearing their stories told through their own words is important. Not only does it reaffirm their basic humanity, it also points to a need to consider a different palette of approaches to violence and poverty and masculinity and nonviolence that might eventually yield enduring results for change.[3]

Though obscuring a face dehumanizes, as Rich notes, obscuring a story relinquishes one's control. So not hearing the obscured voice allows the viewer to cast judgments that fail to consider the life story of a young man who once held hope for the future. Rich continues that without hearing these stories, even well-intentioned caregivers are susceptible to rushing to judgments and developing solutions that are out of sync, ineffective, or even destructive. Allowing a person who is cut dead to share his story not only breaks the bounds of muteness but also gives him the ability to exercise control over how his personhood is regarded.

Kipling Williams writes that control—the ability to fashion one's own story and believe in the possibilities of changing one's future—is linked with human motivation. According to Williams, researchers have found that self-effiency, or belief in one's ability to feel a sense of control in a situation, provides humans strength to persist when failure seems imminent.[4] Given the connections between persistence and motivation, it is not a leap to posit that Nathaniel's lack of ability to "keep faith" in hard times is wed to the lack of control he sensed over changing his condition. In one moment, he regained control by sharing his story and having faith that his story might be heard. After his confession and the long pause of silence, Nathaniel, the mentors, and I stumbled down the road of fearless dialogue. On this journey of authentic sharing, three paradoxical potholes nearly wrecked our attempts at constructive conversation and shattered Nathaniel's sense of control.

Paradox One: I Know You, but I Don't Know You

First, we were *similar but different*. Indeed, Nathaniel, the mentors, and I had the same skin color, and we even shared similar struggles of being muted and made invisible. But, generally, we inhabited disparate worlds. Our backgrounds, education, family structure, age, and conscious and unconscious prejudgments distorted our worldviews, stifled open and honest conversation, and placed us poles apart. These disparate realities led me to question, how can we learn to fully hear and appreciate one another's stories in spite of glaring differences?

Paradox Two: So Close but So Far Away

The second paradox hinges on issues of critical distance—the physical and emotional proximity between the caregiver and the one seeking aid. As stated in the first paradox, it is possible that the caregiver and the unacknowledged person may hail from disparate worlds. However, at the present time, these two unique beings share a common space. Vocational commitments draw many caregivers into spaces that are familiar yet unfamiliar. In such terrain, the caregiver is not fully expert. How, then, does the caregiver bridge the divide when being *in but not a part of* any number of communities?

This paradox evokes questions of how and where the caregiver physically and emotionally situates herself to be of most assistance to those seeking care. It is intriguing that although Nathaniel shared openly, he remained significantly guarded around the issue of family in the one-on-one sessions with me. However, when pushed into a corner in the larger group, he disclosed deeply personal family information pivotal to our successive individual sessions together. This example speaks to not only how assertive or aggressive the caregiver should be in pursuit of change but also where the caregiver situates herself in the care-giving moment. Should the caregiver be distant or connected, close or far away? Or might a third alternative of functioning as an internal critic be most beneficial?

Paradox Three: The Future of No Future

The final paradox centers on conceptions of time and the peculiar notion of living with *the future of no future*. Within many of the young men in Uth Turn, and even in some of the most ambitious students I worked with at Princeton, there existed an eerie discomfort stemming from a belief that they had little control over their future. For these young men, hope was imperiled by the persistent thought of survival in the moment, or their future ambitions were held in balance by grade-granting professors. In fact, one of the most difficult exercises faced by the young men at Uth Turn was outlining future goals; they believed that survival in the streets mandated readied attention to the present moment and that their stigmatized past thwarted any future upward mobility. Nathaniel fit this bill as he, too, was frozen by time. He felt trapped by present circumstances within his family, and lacking viable support networks that could see goodness in him, he found it difficult to "keep faith" that life could be more promising. This stunted view of the future and immobilizing perspective on the past stifles a sense of control. How, then, might caregivers reframe time to promote human flourishing?

In light of these paradoxes, caregivers are challenged to find modes of communication that bridge the gulf of differing life stories, the chasms of emotional and physical distance, and the inhibited perspective of time. Biblical hermeneutics provide helpful resources in constructing a bridge that affirms stories, lessens distance, and allows nimble movement through temporal realities. Particular attention is given to the work of Brian Blount, my mentor, former New Testament professor, and now president of Union Theological Seminary in Richmond, Virginia, who has devoted much of his scholastic career to analyzing how marginal members of society, such as Nathaniel, derive hope and meaning from the biblical story.

Beyond Not Knowing: Internal Digging and Authentic Sharing

"You don't know me!" Nathaniel's words echo the aggressive and confrontational lyrics of southern rapper T.I.'s chart-busting song, "U Don't Know Me." In this song, T.I. dispels the myth that in spite of his cool demeanor and crafty words onstage, he is still a fearless, pistol-shootin', dope-slangin' trapper (i.e., drug dealer) who rarely backs down from confrontation. Much like T.I.'s unwillingness to flee from confrontation, the seemingly levelheaded Nathaniel stood his ground and seized control by exploding with fury when he could no longer tolerate the prejudice and verbal bullying of the Uth Turn mentors. In retrospect, Nathaniel's point was not unfounded, because the impasse between him and the mentors was provoked by a lack of shared understanding and mutual respect for one another's stories. Nathaniel was right. We didn't know him, and it is safe to say that he didn't know us.

In spite of my own feelings of being muted and invisible, in the Uth Turn world, I had privilege, power, and control. As such, to Nathaniel and his peers, I was a person of suspicious origins. I was a thirty-year-old, middle-class, southern-born doctoral student at Princeton Theological Seminary who had no criminal record. Like many of my counselees at Uth Turn, Nathaniel was more than ten years younger than I, he had done poorly in school, and the clutches of poverty in the northeastern United States had led him into a life of criminal activity. In addition, my sacrifices for family paled in comparison to Nathaniel's gritty decision to protect his sisters at his own mother's expense. As African Americans, we shared a minority status, but we were indeed from different worlds.

Strikingly, however, these nuanced differences were also apparent in my talks with African American seminary and undergraduate students at Princeton. Among these African American students, a hierarchal deference was accorded to doctoral candidates, such that transparent conversations and full disclosure were rare. Therefore, whether I was working in Newark or Princeton, considerable effort was necessary to build rapport, to promote shared understanding, and to create an environment for honest exchange.

Interpretive Digs: Caregiver's Internal Probing

Prior to engaging in conversation, a preliminary interpretive step is necessary for serving those with divergent generational, cultural, and socioeconomic life experiences. This initial interpretive move is largely internal. It requires the caregiver to understand the stories of others as an extension of oneself.

Fearless dialogue levels the field by viewing every person's story as worthwhile and personally informative. Given the paradox of knowing but not knowing the person seeking care, the caregiver is challenged to enter conversation with a mind-set that the life story of the cut dead is an extension of the caregiver's own narrative. In other words, the caregiver must realize that which is most beautiful or repulsive in the cut dead exists somewhere in the deep inner regions of the caregiver's own psyche.

At Uth Turn, I had the *privilege* of working with clients who had gang-raped preteen girls remorselessly, carried out assassination-style shootings cavalierly, and beaten elderly addicts with little thought. Hearing these stories was like choking down noxious gases, but as caregiver, I was given entrée into a world unspoken and foreign unto me. However, I attempted not to walk around in the foreign lands of different narratives as a tourist enamored of unfamiliar sites, as a moviegoer entertained by gore, or as a missionary paternalistically placing judgment in search of moralistic resolution. While in the foreign lands of another's story, like an archaeologist I dug around my unconscious searching for points of resonance. Infrequently, I stumbled upon an emotion that allowed me to fully hear the pain of the young man before me. More often I unearthed points of resonance in my dreams. At a visceral and intrapsychic level, I came to relate more to their pain than to the superficial distinctions between us. Lubavitcher Rebbe, a prominent Hasidic rabbi, comments on this notion of repressions as a common denominator to unite seemingly divergent persons:

> The basis by which I can listen to people's problems, sins, and worries is that I can always look into myself and find a disposition for the same problem within me. The last [pious congregant] I listened to told me such a heinous story that I could not find any similarity to his life within me. And upon that realization, I was mortified, because this not only meant that such a similarity did exist, but that it lay deeply repressed within me.[5]

Learning to hear others' problems with an ear to our own repressions alerts the caregiver to the connective tissues among humanity. Although I found it inadvisable to fully disclose and voice these shared understandings of pain for fear of sounding patronizing, the awareness of the pain in me attuned me to hear the stories of the young men at Uth Turn (and from other settings) less judgmentally. Entering each conversation from the vantage point that "what is most repulsive in others mirrors some fragment in me" prepares the caregiver to listen nonjudgmentally and to value life stories that are different but in some way similar to one's own.

Interpretive Dives: Sociolinguistics and Shared Contexts of Meaning

As I plumbed the depths of my own psyche in search of common ground, I realized that the differences between me and the young men at Uth Turn were far greater than educational and socioeconomic disparities. We spoke different languages. To fully hear their stories, it was imperative to join around a common language. In reflecting on the need for a common language, Rich proposes that caregivers must occupy a space in the conversation that "is not so much to judge [the young men's] actions as good or bad, sensible or senseless, as to hear from them and understand how and why they arrive in these perilous places."[6] Sociolinguistic theory—the study of language in relation to social factors—aids caregivers in developing methods to grasp unfamiliar language and to move toward places of shared understanding. The uncanny methods of sociolinguistic theory are central to fearless dialogue and discerning how and why African American young men who feel cut dead end up in perilous places.

Blount contends that distinctive groups must come to understand and appreciate the other's interpretive point of view by learning how the other uses language.[7] In *Cultural Interpretations*, Blount explains the necessity of hearing others in their own voice and in their own language. He states:

> If the marginal members and insiders of society were to come together to discuss a text, there would be no guarantee that one side would hear the concerns of the other. Each side uses a different language, approaches the text from a different linguistic perspective. If one side is to understand the other, it cannot simply listen to what the other says in terms of its own language; it must see the text from the other's sociolinguistic perspective. In other words, it must grasp the other's use of language.[8]

From this perspective, the breakdown in communications is not solely a result of differing sociological factors but is also a result of different linguistic forms.[9] Therefore, the gap between persons or communities in conversation may have as much to do with language differences as with cultural ones. Blount references sociolinguistics as a tool to move divergent interpretive communities to a shared context of meaning.

Sociolinguistics is largely about making subconscious predictions. In biblical exegesis and pastoral consultations alike, biblical scholars and pastoral caregivers are expected to reconstruct written and verbal stories. Subconscious predictions are often most accurate when maximum consideration is given to the situational and cultural environment. For example, in many conversations, "we know what the other person is going to say. We always have a good idea of what is coming next, so that we are seldom totally surprised."[10] So, communicants within a given culture make use of a close relationship between the text and the context to establish the ground for successful communication.

But as cultures differ, so do the subtle clues in language that drive subconscious predictions. Sociolinguistics then provides tools to predict more accurately, and therefore to understand, what the other intends to say and mean. These tools are vital to caregivers challenged to reconstruct stories from piecemeal and eventually represent them in more hopeful ways.

To capture the essence of stories told by marginalized persons, the work of M. A. K. Halliday's functional linguistic theory proves beneficial. Halliday's theory posits that the sociocultural environment of the writer or speaker plays a determinative role in interpreting language and acquiring meaning.[11] In an effort to illustrate that meaning is associated as much with context (how the language is used) as it is with culture (the infrastructure of language), Halliday examines the patterns of language acquisition in children versus the language patterns of adults. Cognizance of these patterns of language is a tool for caregivers to hear marginalized communities in new and unique ways.

According to Halliday, children communicate through seven distinct linguistic stages: instrumental, regulatory, social interaction, personal, heuristic, imaginative, and the representational.[12] In the earlier stages of Halliday's model, children engage their environment in order to communicate with others, while in the latter stages, language is employed to explore and create. Halliday, however, suggests that adults seldom move beyond the penultimate representational stage, which uses language solely to transfer vital information. Hence, a major breakdown in communication results when adults fail to engage the remaining six linguistic functions.

For adults to understand young people and how they comprehend reality, they must not communicate solely from a representational perspective and expect those who are younger to adapt. Rather, adults must seek to understand and ascertain the linguistic components in which younger people derive meaning: "To understand the world as the child understands it, we must comprehend the world from the child's linguistic perspective. Linguistic meaning has a critical contextual component."[13]

To be clear, I am not suggesting that the young men at Uth Turn and the masses who are cut dead communicate in childish, immature, and elementary ways. I am, however, suggesting that a communicative gulf exists unless caregivers employ diverse tools to hear those who may not communicate solely from a representational level. Fearless dialogue rests upon allowing all parties to speak in their most authentic voice. If that voice is not representational, but is regulatory or imaginative, a platform must be developed for its hearing.

In revisiting the New Year's Eve meeting with Nathaniel, it is worthy to note that in recounting John 21, he imaginatively personified the faithful fisherman. His metaphor afforded us the opportunity to speak heuristically and to explore regions of his inner world not previously discussed. Once in this imaginative and heuristic sphere, together we examined: How did his lifestyle coincide with that of a first-century fisherman? Was the fisherman an intriguing image because he experienced the disappointment of not achieving a goal? Recalling Nathaniel's previous statements in our conversation we asked: Did he relate to the fisherman's initial efforts of diligent work without recognition or gain? Was his declarative statement, "I'm not gonna do it," connected to suspicion of the shore-side onlooker, who, like his counselor, may not fully understand the travails of his situation and therefore cannot be trusted for advice? Or was his declaration solely a reference to a lack of faith in himself? These questions were not generated from representational, fact-finding conversation. Fearless dialogue emerges from hearing the expert stories of the cut dead in their own voice, leads from behind, and pushes the previously muted to uncover a truth that always rested within them (more on "leading from behind" and imaginative routes to truth-sharing in chapter 5). Following is one more example of achieving shared understanding through sociolinguistic methods.

After the dust cleared from Nathaniel's outburst, my colleague Torry Winn and I started a six-week workshop called the Better Brother Series. In it, we worked with the Uth Turn participants to choose three of their favorite movies and three of their favorite songs for critical analysis.[14] What emerged from this exercise was poignant. It turns out that each of the selected media had a narrative framework in which the clients identified deeply with the characters and events and seamlessly inserted themselves into their virtual world. One particular week, we pushed play on the stereo and the room erupted. Lost in the song's lyrics, the young men stood on their feet, bobbed their heads, waved their hands, and repeated every word of Lil Wayne's song "Hustla Musik." It was their anthem. Later conversations revealed that this particular song inflamed their aggressions and prepared them psychologically for fisticuffs and gunplay. As the song's plot neared a particularly climactic moment, we pushed stop. Silence.

After hearing the song, the young men were placed in small discussion groups. Because some Uth Turn participants were not strong readers, to alleviate anxiety, no handouts were given and nothing was written down. In these groups, the young men were invited to place themselves in the role of the song's character, examine the character's conflict, and share how they might resolve the character's dilemma. Finally, groups were asked to consider the ramifications behind their decision-making. The Better Brother approach to dialogue acknowledged the countercultural linguistic patterns of the young men at Uth Turn. Employing Halliday's categories, the coded language in rap music employs regulatory and personal linguistic functions, just as the personifications of characters take on an imaginative role.

To enter into fearless dialogue and maneuver around the paradoxical pothole of *knowing but not knowing* the person seeking care, the caregiver must mine her own interior and creatively expand her usage of language. These are merely preliminary steps in hearing the previously muted and cut dead. However, even under the most ideal circumstances, communication may grind into a silent stalemate when power differentials rear their heads. In such instances, organic caregivers must move between margin and center to revive fearless dialogue.

Beyond the Distance: Flowers, Rainbows, and Organic Caregivers

As has been demonstrated in the previous section, the cut dead have much to teach the internally probing caregiver. But from the question "What can I learn from you?" Uth Turn participants (who feel on the margins) inquire whether senior mentors (occupying the center) have transferable skills and life lessons worth learning. At times this gulf between margin and center seemed so vast and bottomless that any conversation involving education or criminal behavior led to confrontation and was stalemated at the aforementioned question. Cracking the deadlocks of seemingly impenetrable stalemates requires a shared distribution of power in dialogue.

For fearless dialogue to flower, caregivers must create a space in which all voices are heard regardless of perceived power or the lack thereof. In *Teaching to Transgress*, cultural critic bell hooks explains that meaningful dialogue emerges in spaces where all voices are heard and everyone's presence is acknowledged.

For hooks, the insistence on an equitable balance of power cannot merely be stated; the facilitator or caregiver must ensure that the presence of every person involved in conversation is valuable. Creating such a space requires deconstruction of the traditional notion that all knowledge rests in the hands of the powerful.[15] Instead, the stories of marginal voices must be brought to center stage and spotlighted as wisdom that provides added depth and new insight to the conversation at hand. Cultural hermeneutics—a field of study that analyzes how cultural backgrounds influence interpretation, particularly the interpretation of texts—is a helpful tool in shifting marginal voices to the center. Blount's approach to multivalent interpretation serves as a model to create spaces where the marginalized voices of the cut dead may be heard among those deemed to be at the center.

Multivalent Interpretation

Blount proposes that just as human circumstances are constantly changing, so are textual interpretations changing. Of course, the text remains the same, but it is multivalent and has many meanings.[16] Under such parameters, it is possible to view any human situation from a myriad of angles. Likewise, any one text has so many meanings that "no single, final interpretation of a text can bring out all of its meaning past, contemporary, and future."[17] If the text is multivalent and interpretations are limitless, then it is advisable to invite multiple interpretative voices into dialogue to inform one another on the text or, in the case of the caregiver, to welcome others to consider the confounding dilemma at hand. Through this approach, each voice lends a different and valuable perspective. However, in spaces where all interpretations are not genuinely valued and recognized, voices—particularly marginal ones—are passed over.

Multivalent interpreters face daunting challenges in seeking to include marginal voices in traditional spaces, where voices at the center dominate. In Blount's field of New Testament studies, he maintains that some interpretations are deemed as more valuable than others and create a restrictive rather than an inclusive environment for conversation. He explains that marginal groups who live outside the value systems of the Eurocentric perspective are often expected to appropriate and adapt their individual circumstances to Eurocentric interpretive norms.[18] Failure to adapt to these norms places alternative or marginal interpreters at risk of being viewed suspiciously, discredited, or made invisible. Certainly, restrictive interpretations are not limited to the academy, for, as seen in Nathaniel's case, holding a countering perspective to powerful mentors subjected him to public discrediting. (Chapter 4 also examines the case of Art, a young man publicly shunned and made invisible for holding a perspective counter to that of his professor.) In restrictive environments, Blount finds it necessary for scholars, and I might add caregivers, interested in creating more inclusive dialogue, to function organically.

Organic Intellectuals and Caregivers

An organic intellectual, for Blount, is highly sensitive to how the language patterns of a culture affect the values and meanings of the powerful and the powerless. In order to bring divergent and stalemated groups into conversation, the organic intellectual must be malleable and decipher how distinctive communities come to different interpretive meanings based on their context. This type of intellectual differs from the characteristic biblical interpreter who seeks to amplify a text's meaning in light of its past context, or the characteristic caregiver who limits her purview to focusing on past faults or seemingly "errant decisions" without hearing the full story. The organic intellectual, Blount says, does not merely record historical struggles but actively works to change them by engaging in dialogue. To foster this dialogue, the organic intellectual must navigate issues of critical distance.

The organic intellectual, who prizes inclusive dialogue, must negotiate her commitment to hearing and amplifying marginal voices. In so doing, she engages in the struggle of the marginalized by highlighting how their culturally sensitive readings provide life-giving meaning to age-old texts or understandings of the world. In this way, organic intellectuals who think multivalently try

> to level the interpretive playing field not only by pointing out that all readings are culturally located and therefore on that basis "equal"; [she] also presses the cause of the reading made by the less empowered community to ensure that it has a proper hearing as an effective and meaningful way of reading text.[19]

Thus, the organic intellectual or caregiver builds a bridge of dialogue by advocating that voices from the margins should be given full voice.

As a bridge-builder for fearless dialogue, the caregiver must multitask. On one hand, the organic intellectual or caregiver dedicates considerable attention to how people on the margin interpret texts and situations from their distinctive perspectives. On the other hand, this bridge-builder must exercise care in not idealizing the voices on the margin at the expense of more dominant inside voices. For instance, a multivalent-minded caregiver might have calmed the scalding mentors and ensured that Nathaniel had an opportunity to voice the reasons behind his criminal actions. However, the intervening caregiver would be careful not to privilege Nathaniel's voice to the extent that the mentors' opinions were silenced. In spaces of fearless dialogue, where hot-button issues teeter on the brink of detonating rage, the organic intellectual or caregiver moves between margin and center to assure that all parties are afforded equal hearing. Blount colorfully refers to this volatile dialogue of multiple interpretations as "a rainbow of potential meaning whose individual colors, while visible to one interpreter or community, are invisible to many others."[20]

Rainbows of Potential Meaning

In order to gain access to the rainbow's fullest spectrum of textual meaning, a multitude of communal interpretations must be engaged. Analysis is not limited to one interpreter or to a single group of interpreters. The complete rainbow becomes visible when all parties have equal representation in the dialogue.

Nathaniel was not afforded equal representation in the conversation at Uth Turn. The mentors dominated the conversation, relegated Nathaniel's voice to the margins, and made the appearance of a rainbow of potential meaning bleak. However, Nathaniel's self-disclosure shifted the power dynamics in the room. The faithful sharing of his narrative placed him squarely at the center, causing all in attendance to reinterpret the motives behind his criminal behavior and possibly to reexamine their own "errant" decision-making. In this shift of power a rainbow did appear.

For many casual bystanders, rainbows after a summer rain are delightful matters of chance; however, for seasoned organic caregivers, rainbows of potential meaning that appear after stormy stalemates are invaluable sites of growth. Unfortunately, I was not seasoned enough to maximize the potential learning opportunity after Nathaniel's explosive disclosure. However, in the fictive account below, I share how a more seasoned organic caregiver might have seized the moment.

Rewind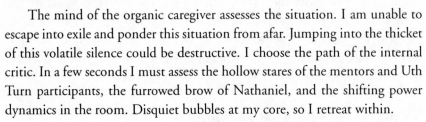

NATHANIEL: You don't know me! My mom's a crackhead. I got two younger sisters. My mom used to prostitute out of our house to get money for crack. I started selling drugs to my mom to protect my sisters from the men coming in our house.

Silence fell upon the room.

Slow Motion

The mind of the organic caregiver assesses the situation. I am unable to escape into exile and ponder this situation from afar. Jumping into the thicket of this volatile silence could be destructive. I choose the path of the internal critic. In a few seconds I must assess the hollow stares of the mentors and Uth Turn participants, the furrowed brow of Nathaniel, and the shifting power dynamics in the room. Disquiet bubbles at my core, so I retreat within.

In the split seconds of inner probing, I feel Nathaniel's pain of hurting a loved one to save a loved one. Although it reeks of ethical relativism, the mentors are humanizing this young man. Perhaps they even shed a layer of their thoughts on original sin and come to see that these young men may not be innately flawed but deeply altruistic. From the quizzical gaze of the Uth Turn participants, I gather that some of the young men are calculating the risks of sharing their own stories to gain greater visibility and voice.

In the room, I feel pain and hope. But as a multivalent interpreter, I must ensure that every person has an opportunity to speak. Careful not to miss the potential rainbow of interpretation, the organic caregiver and internal critic might say something like this:

Play

Silence is a gift from God, and so is chaos. In silence we hear ourselves, and in the destruction of chaos space is cleared to build new understanding. I am certain I am not the only one who feels pain and is rebuilding a new understanding of family and sacrifice. What can we learn from this moment, this brother's story? There's no wrong answer. If Nathaniel is comfortable, I'd invite him speak first. Then, I invite anyone in the room who feels comfortable to answer that same question. What can we learn from this moment? Let's speak fearlessly. If no one chooses to speak, let us learn from the silence, the chaos, the new beginnings breaking forth.

As fearless dialogue unfolds, time seems to stand still and a rainbow arches after the silent storm. This leads to the final parameter of fearless dialogue: caregivers must view time fluidly.

Beyond a Future of No Future: Time-Bending Pockets of Resistance

Long before my work at Uth Turn and my doctoral research on cultural hermeneutics and narrative therapies, I learned that stories could bend time and alter how people viewed life. In my boyhood, I recall sitting transfixed at my grandfather's feet while he painted elaborate narratives with words. Intuitively realizing that listeners internalized information differently, his art of storytelling employed broad brushstrokes of oral history accented by song, folklore, proverbs, and prayers. The deep tones of detail captured in his stories colored the canvas of my mind and, years later, still live in me.

I can smell, for instance, the charring wood of the cross burning outside my grandfather's childhood home. Over the sound of crackling wood and whispered prayers, I hear the vitriol and envy dripping from the lips of Klan members hurling epithets at my great-grandfather, Papa Caesar, a prosperous black farmer. I choke on the thick Mississippi air as Papa Caesar and his family escape under the cover of nightfall by carthorse, a straw-filled mattress concealing the few valuables they could muster in the rapid move. Connected by story, I feel the thick droplets of blood fall from Grandpa's teenaged hands and color the patch of cotton whose spiny thorns raked his open palm. Even still I hear voices, the owner of the land he sharecropped, "Short again!" The discontented scream of Mama Dinah, "Leave now!" after learning that her son, my grandfather, had hit that landowner. I am in the room, eavesdropping on the prayers of Grandpa's family and friends before his exodus: "May the Good Lord bless you, boy." I finally hear the impassioned whisper of my grandfather to his new bride before his flight north, "No kids of ours ever gone pick a piece of cotton."

Grandpa's story lives in me today because its telling exploded the parameters of time in my boyish mind. This family history recast a seemingly tragic past into a story of triumph over adversity. Drawn into the timeless orb of the story, I experienced an immanent God carving out vestiges of hope in a situation shrouded with despair. In Grandpa's parting words to his bride, I saw my own life wrapped in a young couple's future vision. By story's end I felt strangely moved to walk boldly in the present, knowing that in those storied moments I had been divinely touched and had transcended the bounds of time.

Constrained by the limits of time and a burdensome life story, countless African American young men who feel cut dead stagger in the world. They lack a captive audience to hear and reframe the pains of yesteryear, and for them, the yoke of the past becomes an albatross. The steps of the current day are beleaguered by stigma and stereotype, and the ever-present strain of mere survival makes future casting an unbearable load. Unable to lift the veil of the past or see beyond the present moment, these young men lose control of time, and their future becomes no future. However, in pockets of fearless dialogue, the God of eternity releases the trappings of time and transforms the past into a site of wisdom, the present into a space of resistance, and the future into a world of radical possibility. Blount's study of the book of Mark serves as a valuable resource to examine how the kingdom of God bursts into the present to shift temporal realities and to catalyze change.

Pockets of the Kingdom Introduced

Traditional Christian eschatology, or the doctrine of end things, posits that Christ will come from universal glory and judge the world. This traditional notion of the end-times casts human flourishing deep into the future and may lead some in the present to feel apathetic and hopeless.[21] A realized eschatology, however, contends that the presence of God actively works in tandem with human action to transform present sociohistorical realities. Blount's *Go Preach! Mark's Kingdom Message and the Black Church Today* analyzes how these glimpses of the Kingdom were perceptible in the boundary-breaking ministry of Jesus and are discernible today.

The kingdom of God, in Blount's terms, is a transcendent space created through human action and divine intervention.[22] When these forces align, the future kingdom forcibly and miraculously pierces into the present moment to overturn oppressions of the present age.[23] Blount calls these kingdom in-breaking moments that alter time "pockets of resistance." These pockets have power and far-reaching implications, he explains:

Mark's kingdom language communicates the projection of a supernatural power that intervenes in human life and history. The symbol is *spiritual* because it demands a kind of interior trust, a belief that the kingdom whose reality is flashed into the present as a pocket moment will ultimately be consummated in full. It is *social* because it inspires believers to provoke other such pocket manifestations in their contemporary social and political histories. It is therefore both soteriological and political. Its *soteriological* goal is every bit as encouraging of *socio-political* activism as it is of redemptive spirituality. In fact, it is my contention that kingdom calls, which on the surface appear to have a singular orientation, also have dramatic socio-political implication.[24]

From this description, one gathers that when pockets of resistance pierce into the present, they elicit internal and external, individual and sociopolitical change. Pockets of resistance explode into reality when fearless dialogue reaches its precipice. Although these moments may finitely be measured in seconds, the epiphanies ascertained are timeless, for in them is power to humanize the dejected, to catalyze acts of justice, and to visualize the Incarnate in the cut dead. Pockets of resistance lie before us like altars in the world; we only need eyes to see them and courage to seize these gateways to the kingdom. A closer look at the boundary-breaking ministry of Jesus heightens vision and provides a model of recreating these pockets.

Boundary-Breaking Care

In the sociopolitical community in which Mark penned his Gospel, the people of Israel were persecuted by Roman authorities, just as their enslaved Hebrew ancestors suffered under Egyptian rule. The Israelites had just witnessed the end of a terrible war and the fall of the Jewish temple in 70 C.E. Under Roman domination, Mark's readers anticipated the coming of a militaristic Messiah, whose singular purpose would be to overthrow Rome through violent revolution. In this politically charged atmosphere, countless messiah figures and false prophets claimed to possess powers that could topple the Roman Empire in order to erect God's kingdom.[25] As Mark's readers stood ready for revolt, Mark presented a Messiah whose view of the kingdom and of revolution was quite different.

Although "messianic revolutionaries proclaimed that war was God's actual intervention into human history to reestablish an independent Jewish state,"

Mark spoke of a kingdom that intervened to destroy nationalistic behaviors opposed to God's ways.[26] For Mark, God was not seeking to replicate Israel's past and overthrow Caesar, as God had overthrown Pharaoh. Nor was God seeking to create another Davidic kingdom that constantly failed to meet divine ideals of communal living. Instead, God's intervention was to reform Israel and to build a kind of community "whose inner focus on justice would be a transforming and inviting beacon for all the world."[27] Since building community was such a central theme for Mark, it comes as no surprise that the Messiah would institute a kingdom that shattered superficial boundaries and humanized those deemed to be of "impure" pedigree.[28]

A boundary-breaking Messiah was needed not only to check the power-hungry Roman authorities but also to give visibility and voice to those cut dead within Israel's own community. For within the house of Israel, economic disparities favored the wealthy and devalued the poor. Holiness codes declared that the circumcised who observed the Sabbath and followed a kosher diet were healthy and pure. Thus, the Gentiles and those who lacked optimal health (i.e., lepers, the lame, and the blind) were considered impure and unholy.[29] Legal boundaries compounded division as the broken and infirm were socially ostracized and unable to attain the healing and wholeness they sought. In a climate not strikingly different from that experienced by stigmatized African American young men, who are stereotyped as vagrantly impure and separated from society as social junk or social dynamite, the Markan Jesus breaks into human history, creates pockets of resistance, and shatters boundaries through three manifestations of preaching: teaching, exorcism, and healing.

The Markan Jesus teaches. Like the seamless recounting of time and limitless meanings present in my grandfather's allegory, Jesus' teaching of parables is perhaps the most obvious place to decipher pockets bursting into human life. For instance, Mark's Jesus stands in earshot of an agrarian crowd—who tangibly knew the qualities of good and bad soil, as well as the pains of internal division and persecution—teaching the parable of the sower.[30] The familiarity of the image and the visceral feelings of inner disruption and outer exclusion invited the listeners into an alternate sphere much like what I experienced as a boy. Fully entrenched in the parable, but fully cognizant of the difficulties in the world around them, those hearing the parable would glimpse the future but not be torn from the present. Moreover,

Blount proclaims that this irruption of the new age into the old demands that the hearers of the parable make a choice about how they will respond to Jesus' teaching (or sowing).[31] The hearer is forced to choose which kind of soil he or she will be—one of obedient discipleship that brings life and builds community or one of derision that fortifies existing boundaries.

The Markan Jesus exorcises. Blount exegetes a pericope in the first chapter of Mark (verses 23-27), in which Jesus is confronted after teaching authoritatively to a man with an unclean spirit. For Blount, this mythological standoff redirects Mark's readers to the fact that "Jesus represents God's intervention in human time."[32] The in-breaking presence of the divine forces the unclean spirit out of the man and sends a message to onlookers that God can and will intervene victoriously over forces that antagonize individual and communal peace.[33] Awestruck by what they had witnessed, the onlookers *go preach* to others of the divine powers they had seen.

Pockets of resistance isolate and attack forces that threaten wholeness and peace. Prior to his explosive disclosure, Nathaniel was tormented by death-dealing voices that labeled him solely as a "troublemaker" and a hardened "drug dealer." In the space of fearless dialogue, a pocket moment was created for him to exorcise his demons and for once to be seen as a human crying for help. Like the onlookers in the synagogue after the exorcism, the people who witnessed Nathaniel's self-disclosure grasped the gravity of the moment. Weeks later, the Better Brother Series was born, and young men who had witnessed Nathaniel's reaping felt more comfortable to share their own life stories and exorcise their own demons. Like the first-century onlookers, they felt compelled to *go preach* in hopes of attaining a different reality.

The Markan Jesus heals. According to Blount, the healing of the leper is one of Jesus' most dramatic boundary-breaking moments (Mark 1:40-43). Jesus touches the leper and heals him. Once healed, the leper takes up the mantle of preaching. Simple enough? Not so.

Jesus' touch breaks boundaries. Jesus touches the leper and breaches a cultic code. Jesus heals the castigated leper and restores him into community.[34] Finally, the healed leper, who once was on the margin, becomes a voice who speaks truth from the margins to the center.

Miraculous healings that break some physical law of nature may seem implausible to the modern reader. However, "contemporary miracles need not have the explosiveness of a storm quelled or an illness removed to make transformative waves." Small miracles that shift the trajectories of human lives explode upon the expanse of time daily. These tiny miracles break contemporary cultic codes and humanize those seen as possessing little worth. Minute miracles restore the cut dead to community. Infinitesimal miracles break in as seeds of hope in fearless dialogue. Strain with me to see these tiny miracles bursting forth into the present lives of the young men chronicled hereafter and the caregivers who risk so much to aid them.

A Final Word: *WildKingdom*

Romping through the flatlands of marginality are the young men with troubled brows. Trapped in the cavernous spaces of their inner being are the unresolved issues from their past. Day in and day out, they bear the threat of extinction. It's wild out there; no time to think of the future. In heat, well-meaning predators infringe upon their inner space. Cornered and emotionally stripped bare, for them explosion is immanent. BOOM! The Kingdom bursts forth into reality, ushered in by the calculated risk of being heard. In the silence, downtrodden onlookers feel a transcendent lift, a resurrected sense of control. Choices must be made. Bear the weight of fearless dialogue, or mouse away in timid resignation? They choose the former. But now that they have glimpsed hope, will they lose their minds?

Stillbirth

I was conceived in a moment of passionate
love and freedom

I was born at a funeral, where hope died at my
father's treason

A toddler's nightmares have overtaken my
infantile dreamin'

And the prisons build a cell for me, at 3rd
grade 'cause I ain't readin'

Created by my mother's first love, yet at 15
I'm a second hand citizen; a grievance

—William K. Gravely

THE DEATH OF SELF-ESTEEM AND THE SEED OF AN INTERRUPTING HOPE

Then I looked, and there before me was sulfur falling from the sky.
²My eyes affixed in awe and sheer horror, I scanned the destruction.
³City burning, traffic jamming, children crying, red lights flashing,
looters looting, and one walked calmly with newspaper under arm.
⁴A yellow globule hits my blue car hood, smolders, and liquefies into
a greenish alloy.

The Beast out of the Earth

⁵Then I saw a mechanical beast, coming out of the earth. As I
watched, its long metallic arm laid bare houses and city streets,
delivered fatal wounds to young and old alike. ⁶Transfixed by the
wreckage, I'm oblivious to the glow inside the car. ⁷When I turned, I
saw a mighty angel; "his face was like the sun, and his legs were like
fiery pillars." He gave a shout like the roar of a lion, "The time has
come to meet the Maker." ⁸I exited the vehicle.

Two Witnesses and the Tree of Life

¹⁰I saw not one familiar face, and no one saw me. ¹¹On foot I maneuver
the riotous streets. Guns firing, craps shooting, people running, cars
exploding, incautious copulating, and one sat in resignation waiting

to die. [12]The putrid smell of death fills my lungs. [13]"And there came flashes of lightning, peals of thunder, an earthquake, and a hellacious hailstorm." [14]To the hills for safety, I ascend. An uneasy tranquility, I feel there. [15]A government motorcade passes, to safety I assume; a possibility not afforded my family or me. [16]I saw my parents atop the hill, standing beneath the tree of life and staring down at the beast, the burning wreckage, and the confusion below. [17]Silent tears fall, and so does a yellow droplet that singes a leaf on the tree of life. [18]As the burning leaf crumples like gas-soaked papier-mâché, a seed dislodges. And there before me was a single seed of life falling to earth against a backdrop of golden rain.[1]

Eyes open! Awake now? Full body chills draw me back to consciousness as I peel off damp sheets. Not an ordinary dream, this hair-raising Patmos vision drew me into a foreign world and forced me to reckon with how I would respond to the stresses of imminent death. Imminent death—not an everyday thought for an Ivy League–trained seminary professor. Needless to say, in the face of death, my hope was challenged, and I was impelled to examine my capacity to care in the midst of chaos. For some, conceiving of a life without a future or living with bleak possibilities for flourishing is as foreign as this dream. Not so for Art and Thomas, two young men who lived through nightmarish ordeals yet had the heart to hope.

One spring afternoon in Princeton, a frantic phone call interrupted me from my study: "Hurry, I need you to meet Art at [a local restaurant] for an urgent, crisis counseling session." Such a call for impromptu "informal" counseling was not uncommon, for a number of African American graduate students on the seminary and university campuses had come to know me as an engaged listener who holds confidences and possesses practical wisdom. Most of the students I met were often overstressed and sought guidance on managing and resolving internalized frustrations. However, Art had reached his breaking point and had lashed out at the institution by verbally threatening administrators.

Earlier that day, the twenty-two-year-old Art was informed by his professor that he was receiving a failing grade. Art, a particularly sharp and witty student who was unaccustomed to failure, carried a heavy course load and excelled in his other classes. However, in our impromptu crisis-counseling session, he suggested that, possibly due to ideological differences and contested classroom debates, a communication stalemate emerged between him and his instructor. Art further explained that at some point during the semester, "He stopped hearing me!" Thus, Art's enraged outburst was born out of a sense that he was not given the opportunity to articulate his ideas and, in turn, was failed for being different from and thinking differently than his professor.

Following a series of conversations with me and a local therapist between semesters, Art regained his composure and continued his graduate studies. However, after enduring the effects of being silenced, something noticeably was lost. Though he excelled in his other classes, the failing grade and perceived disrespect of his professor changed his outlook and disposition toward school. As time passed, Art's bright light began to dim, and the once eager and inquisitive student grew more beleaguered and bored with the academy. His willingness and drive to contest ideological differences with colleagues and his professors slowly waned, and the once vibrant student now slept through classes and turned in assignments late. His lethargy was coupled with questions of identity, purpose, and faith, which ultimately led to greater confusion, isolation, and bewilderment. Increasingly introspective and reluctant to speak out in his classes and risk being silenced further, Art sat in resignation. With his self-esteem withering, possibilities for retaining hope would prove challenging.

Over forty miles away from Princeton, and on the other end of the socioeconomic spectrum, lies Newark. I am reminded of my first encounter there with Thomas at a Uth Turn group session. Like Art, Thomas was an African American young man who went to great lengths to be seen and heard. With the staccato southern drawl of rapper T.I. rhyming about "the mistakes made on [his] road to wealth" echoing from my iPod, I began the evening session by reflecting on how life's difficulties aid in the discovery of purpose. To contextualize the session, we analyzed T.I.'s song, and I shared one of the three critical incidents that led me to devote half of my thirty-year life to reinvigorating hope in hopeless African American youth. I divulged to the group that after a high-school basketball game during my sophomore year, a friend since boyhood, who had served as an older brother to me, was punched from behind, pinned to the ground, and shot in the head. Further, I shared that I did not respond with retaliatory violence but worked with administrators in my school to start a peer conflict and mediation council to prevent future violence. "That's b***s***!"[2] Thomas interrupted. This unexpected and frank interruption was an invitation to fearless dialogue and the catalyst to open future conversations between Thomas and me.

In the following weeks, as I learned more about the stresses of Thomas's life, his frank response made more sense to me. He lived a life of deprivation and struggle for survival. During his school-age years, he stole the gifts of his classmates after holiday breaks because his family could not afford to exchange presents. His timely thievery earned him the nickname "Holiday." His growing reputation on the street made him a likely candidate for gang life. The eldest male child but too young to be employed, he participated from the age of eleven in drug-related activities to financially support his family.

For several years Thomas whirled through a vicious cycle of neglect, destabilized by lawless life decisions and a lack of communal resources. This cycle moved him *from* the unstructured chaos of street life *to* an overcrowded juvenile system with little funding for rehabilitation *to* overtaxed public schools with little tolerance for problem students and *back to* the streets again. Thomas attempted to counter the threats to his own visibility in this cycle by responding to the mildest slight as his alter identity, "Holiday," with what I call an "in-your-face, see-me-now" posturing. Such posturing demanded respect, instilled fear, and guaranteed street credibility by threatening physical violence to anyone who disrespected, ignored, or belittled his humanity. The logic of this posturing posits that if you disrespect or ignore me, I will hit you (i.e., with my fist or with my gun) and you will "see me now." In his world of deprivation and survival, he reasoned, if someone hurts you, you instinctively hurt him back. Thus, Thomas later explained to me that he reacted so strongly to my nonretaliatory response to my friend's death because he had never before encountered someone who decided not to avenge the death of a loved one with reciprocal violence.

By the time I spoke with eighteen-year-old Thomas at Uth Turn, he had already done over ten "bids"[3] in correctional facilities for drug-related crimes. Influenced by a few well-meaning individuals who invested time and attention in him during his cycle of neglect, he had attained his GED and was interested in pursuing a college education. Though he was eager to learn and discover new possibilities, Thomas's self-esteem plummeted with the simple mention of his name and the criminal record that stained his résumé. Trapped in the normalized chaos of a community with few resources and inhibited by the stigma of "Holiday," his street name symbolizing the past identity he sought to escape, Thomas desperately foraged for a seed of hope.

Sustained reflection on the experiences of Art and Thomas led me to the realization that though their exterior socioeconomic environments were starkly different, their interior psycho-spiritual struggles were strikingly similar. Both young men found themselves in physical locales where their visibility and voice were contested. Art experienced this as not being "heard" by his professor because of ideological differences. Thomas desired to be seen as someone other than "Holiday," but cycling through a system of neglect, he maneuvered riotous city streets where no one could see him as more.

Pressured by the constricting nature of their physical locations, which contributed to their feelings of muteness and invisibility, both young men sought acknowledgment through aggression (i.e., verbal threats and posturing), much like Parenti's social dynamite. Despite their explosive efforts to gain recognition, both young men felt trapped by their situation and were vulnerable to succumbing to hopelessness. This susceptibility to hopelessness is exemplified as the once intellectually quarrelsome Art resigned himself to lethargic academic disinterest—possibly signifying a transition from a battle-stricken, social-dynamite-like identity to an identity characteristic of Parenti's more withdrawn social junk. Similarly, Thomas, with aspirations for higher education, was stifled by a lack of communal resources and the stigma attached to his alter identity, "Holiday." Perhaps the most pertinent intersection between these two cases is that, at the time of our meeting, both Art and Thomas were seeking a hopeful alternative to lift their self-esteem and move beyond their current situation.

But for Art and Thomas, entertaining hopeful thoughts in the face of imminent mental and physical death was no easy measure. They sought authentic expression but were stripped of their voice. On a quest for autonomy, they were denied visibility. In pursuit of self-betterment, they were cut dead. For them, time was an enemy. The weight of past decisions and age-old labels became an immobilizing albatross. The present normalized chaos, triggered rage, and induced resignation while the future collapsed. Once-lofty goals were transformed to moment-to-moment survival and short-term gambles of risk and reward.

For the cut dead who are trapped in vicious cycles of neglect, hopelessness hovers like clouds of sulfuric rain, nightmares of a dreaded future seep into present reality, and self-esteem shrivels like gas-soaked papier-mâché. As their world crumbles from within, good-hearted caregivers meander into sooty apocalyptic spaces to stand alongside these young men devoid of visibility and voice. Giving little thought to their own hope, these caregivers entrench themselves in the ruins and internalize the toxins of the previously cut dead. Before long, the caregiver's self-esteem begins to wither, vibrancy is transformed into sullenness, and hope begins to wilt. How can caregivers instill hope in others, when they are bereft of hope themselves?

This chapter makes a case for the presence of an interrupting hope to disrupt the loss of self-esteem and to foil the woeful ills of despair, apathy, and shame. The psychological and developmental origins of hope are considered to address the specific needs of African American young men who are cut dead but still alive. The chapter concludes with reflections on the dangers of caring and with the introduction of three allies of hope to empower caregivers in the embattled trenches with the cut dead.

A Loss of Self-Esteem and the Antibody of Interruption

It is a peculiar sensation . . . of always looking at one's self through the eyes of others, of measuring one's soul by the tape of a world that looks on in amused contempt and pity.

—W. E. B. Du Bois, *The Souls of Black Folk*

Imagine how it might feel if every time you looked in the mirror what you saw staring back at you was a stilled face, a confused look, or disdainful eyes.[4] Before long you might recoil from looking into mirrors at all. Many psychologists agree that the face of another is a mirror that reflects back an image of the viewer.[5] However, when the mirroring face of the other reflects back disdain or is so stilted it seems to create no reflection at all, a peculiar sensation emerges that begins to chip at one's self-esteem.

Self-esteem is an "internal gauge or monitor of perceived relational value [that increases] when people feel accepted by others and decreases when people do not."[6] The constant pressure of being overlooked, or even looked at askance, carries the implicit accusation that there is something about the cut dead that is bad or unwanted. Over time, this implicit message of deviance threatens self-esteem and leads to an internalization of the belief that one is undesirable.[7] While high self-esteem holds (unconscious) thoughts of rejection at bay, lower self-esteem may lead one to question one's value in the eyes of others, to internalize rejection, and eventually to withdraw from tasks that may threaten to expose perceived negative qualities.

Self-esteem is most jeopardized when self-analysis is resisted and when help from others is shunned. Internalized feelings of inadequacy destroy an individual's trust in his perceived reality, causing a decreased sense of agency and self-constricted freedom. Painful self-images can cause a person to become "less spontaneous, less free-spirited, more cautious, [and] more calculating."[8] This more calculating disposition reduces risk-taking by making the person less apt to explore new experiences and more prone to invest energy into self-survival. From this constricted view of the world, life becomes narrow, mundane, predictable, and routine.[9] A self-constricted individual is prone to internalize problems, present an omnipotent façade, and mistrust himself and others in addressing the internal site of conflict. Unfortunately, a constricted sense of self not only estranges and limits one's daily freedom, but constriction makes African American young men more susceptible to internal depletion and a loss of self-esteem. An interrupting force is needed to penetrate socially hardened exteriors and unexamined empty cores and to obstruct the nonaffirming gazes that mirror back abnormality.

(Violence) Interrupter

In the most basic sense, to interrupt is to disrupt or stop the continuous progress of an activity or process. Gary Slutkin, the founder of CeaseFire, introduced the novel idea of interrupting violence. Slutkin, a medical doctor who spent most of his career fighting epidemic diseases such as tuberculosis, cholera, and AIDS with the World Health Organization, proposed the idea that the epidemic of violence could be contained like a contagious disease. In a lecture on his approach, Slutkin examines this metaphor by arguing that "characteristics of every epidemic are seen in violence epidemics: infectivity, incubation periods, transmission characteristics, susceptibility, reactivation, and even vertical transmission from adult to child."[10] For Slutkin, the parallel structure of contagious disease and violence is good news because science has developed strategies to stop epidemics. Chief among these strategies is interrupting transmission.

Slutkin explains that in a flu epidemic doctors immunize to block transmission. To block the transmission of violence, Slutkin's organization developed "a cadre of workers called the violence interrupters who can detect and interrupt events and block one of them from leading to another."[11] Like human antibodies,[12] CeaseFire's interrupters have been attacking the disease of violence on the gang-infested streets of Chicago since 2004. Commissioned to douse heated quarrels on the front end, violence interrupters interject themselves into potential powder kegs of lethal dispute and smother conflict before matters get out of hand.[13]

In an award-winning *Frontline* documentary entitled *The Interrupters*, viewers are taken into volatile spaces to observe how CeaseFire's staff actually blocks the transmission of violence before it escalates. One particular scene shows the diminutive yet fiery Ameena Matthews encircled by over a dozen raging teenage men set on retaliation after the death of a close friend. Stepping beyond the edge of a young man's personal space, Matthews stands within inches of his face and declares how unacceptable it is for her to be holding the slain boy's obituary. After asserting that schools, churches, and their momma's houses were safe zones that should be free from shooting, she shares with them a glimpse of her own past of street fighting and criminal behavior. With the attentive eyes of the surrounding teenagers focused on Matthews at the core of the circle, she pulls a preteen to the center of the circle and asks:

> Who does this baby belong to? . . . He just hanging around y'all. He sees everything you all do, right? So if this brother catch a case and do 100 years, whose fault is it? Is it his fault? . . . Teach him righteous. Y'all got it? Y'all got it? [Then turning to the oldest member of the crew, she states:] I'm looking to you.[14]

In this incident, Matthews stands literally in the center of conflict and proposes a stopgap, a moment of reflection in the midst of rage. Easily misconstrued as an adult lecturing young people, Matthews is a "credible messenger"[15] engaging in fearless dialogue by asking questions and having the young men consider the consequences of their actions. Chief among her questions is the generative inquiry about who will take responsibility for the "baby." This interruption of violence challenged the young men to take ownership of their actions and to be fully cognizant of the consequences.

After a three-year evaluation of the CeaseFire program, statistics showed that from the work of the violence interrupters shootings decreased 16 to 28 percent in four of the seven regions studied in some of Chicago's toughest neighborhoods.[16] So compelling were these findings that the program has been replicated in Los Angeles, New Orleans, and even Trinidad and Iraq. Given the success and international reach of CeaseFire's model, is it possible for caregivers to serve as psychic interrupters who disrupt the transmission of virulent hopelessness? This is only possible if interrupting caregivers are open to interruption.

The Invitation of Interruption

In *Reaching Out*, Henri Nouwen speaks of interruptions as gifts for caregivers who are preoccupied with change and harried by ever-growing demands. Nouwen begins his reflection on this subject by recounting a moment during his professorship at the University of Notre Dame, when he received some untimely wisdom from a senior colleague. While strolling across campus, the older professor shared, "You know, my whole life I have been complaining that my work was constantly interrupted, until I discovered that my interruptions were my work."[17] From the wise professor's vantage point, interruptions are small opportunities to break from the mundane and create new possibilities. Nouwen adds that unexpected interruptions might even be considered as invitations to contest "old-fashioned and outmoded styles of living"[18] and as ways to explore uncharted areas of experience.

In unforeseen circumstances, interruptions invite caregivers into spaces of chaos and turmoil to interrupt cycles of hopelessness in others. However, the caregiver must be ready to accept the unexpected invitation when it comes. When prepared to receive the gift of an interruption, caregivers "can look for hope in the middle of crying cities, burning hospitals, and desperate parents."[19] In the words of Nouwen, caregivers "can cast off the temptation of despair and *speak about the fertile tree while witnessing the dying seed.*"[20] Or, in the case of caregivers working with the cut dead in apocalyptic dead zones, one can speak about the dying tree of life releasing the fertile seed of an interrupting hope.

An Interrupting Hope Defined

An interrupting hope is a disrupting desire for existential change that is generated and sustained in a community of reliable others that names difficulties, envisions new possibilities, and inspires work toward transformation of self and other. The constant negotiation between self and other and the navigation among narrative, time, and space make hope a journey and not a static philosophical belief. Predicated upon movement to change, an interrupting hope is more like a pilgrimage, during which the cut dead and the caregiver are transformed along the way.

Some sense of felt need prompts the first step into the wilderness of change. Psychologists have stated that for hope to exist there must first be some sense of captivity or deprivation.[21] Far from idle fantasy, hope is grounded in the sense that something of great importance is lacking. This sense of deprivation may come from something lost: good health, a meaningful relationship, or an opportunity for meaningful work. However, it may manifest itself as a deeply personal lacking that is difficult to articulate. For instance, one stricken by personal inadequacy may sense that life is unfulfilling and devoid of purpose or that in spite of natural giftedness one lacks adequate resources to succeed. Deprivations have the power both to disrupt the entire self and to catalyze a hope that seeks to capture what is missing in life.[22] While deprivations internally trigger hope, outside forces are also catalyzing agents.

This definition exemplifies that hope is generated in a community of reliable others. While I examine the origins of the community of reliable others in a later section and devote the final chapter to its supportive role in the life of the previously unacknowledged, it is important to note that hope is not derived in isolation. Even for the most hopeful persons there are times "when our purely inward resources are not enough."[23] Hope is born out of collaborative interchange. For example, an individual who feels deprived of meaning may be inspirited to hope after reading an account in the Sunday newspaper of a villager in a war-torn township who overcame incomparable difficulties to survive. I offer this example because the community of reliable others that generates hope may not always be physically present. Instead, this community may be any combination of textual, scriptural, historical, or even virtual supports.[24] In any event, its presence is felt and the seed that there is a possibility for existential change is planted.

This community of reliable others elicits action in the individual striving for existential change. Hope thrives in an environment of accountability that does not sidestep current challenges or recoil into fatalistic thinking. Instead, the individual and community face present difficulties and envision future possibilities together. This relationship between individual and community is mutually formative, making the pursuit of hope a generative and risky endeavor that transforms self and other. I return to and expand upon this definition throughout the remainder of the book, but one may wonder what distinguishes hope as interruptive.

Interruption lies at the heart of hope and is the bloodline pulsing through this entire book. An interrupting hope is a stopgap that reroutes the toxic flow of rage and nihilism that erode a hopeful outlook on life. Interrupting hope encourages those denied visibility and voice to disruptively speak, while emboldening caregivers to move confidently between margin and center and to foster fearless dialogue. This interrupting hope shatters temporal realities, allowing for pockets of resistance to penetrate human action and to create miraculous solutions in which problems were seemingly intractable before. An interrupting hope looks danger squarely in the eye and believes that in tandem with a community of reliable others, the pursuit of visibility, voice, and existential change outweighs the threat of psychic harm or physical death. An interrupting hope that is unflinching in the face of risk emerges from obscure origins.

Beyond the Origins of Hope: A Developmental Examination of Hope

In the opening paragraph of *Agents of Hope,* pastoral theologian Donald Capps says, "What pastors have uniquely to give others is hope. . . . To be a pastor is to be a provider or agent of hope."[25] This statement suggests that a pastor possesses a unique worldview inclining her to see life's difficulties through a distinctive lens in order to present new possibilities to those devoid of hope. If hope is, indeed, the pastor's or caregiver's primary resource, this caregiver should have a working knowledge of the allies and threats to hope. Likewise, caregivers must possess a fundament of hope themselves. But what if this is not the case and the caregiver dispensing vestiges of hope to others does so from an empty place? Is it possible that the emptiness is the result of hope never fully developing in the earliest stages of life? If so, is all hope for maintaining a hopeful outlook lost? For answers to these queries, we turn to expert voices who have considered the origins of hope.

Erik Erikson: Infantile Hope

Erik Erikson, a German-born American psychologist and psychoanalyst most noted for his research on psychosocial development, locates the genesis of the hopeful self in infancy. In what some consider his most decisive article on hope, "Human Strength and the Cycle of Generations," Erikson locates the development of an attitude of hope in the earliest stages of infancy and suggests that as the hopeful self matures, so does a religious view of life. In this article, Erikson expounds on his groundbreaking life cycle theory, which maintains that healthy human development consists of eight developmental stages. With successful passage through each developmental stage, a corresponding human strength or virtue is gained. The first stage of Erikson's life cycle is marked by tensions between trust and mistrust. Healthy development through this stage generates the virtue of hope.[26]

For Erikson, hope is the "enduring belief in the attainability of fervent wishes, in spite of dark urges and rages which mark the beginning of existence."[27] This definition suggests that hope exists and becomes manifest in preverbal interactions between the infant and the care-giving adult. Caught in the tensions of emerging senses of trust and mistrust, the infant optimally places trust in the "care-giving person" who responds affirmatively to the infant's physical and emotional needs. As the infant's needs are regularly met, trust comes to be fostered in other persons and in the surrounding world. If needs are met and hoped-for events come to pass, the infant will continue to entrust himself to others. From these early experiences of affirmation, the virtue of hope continues to emerge as a basic quality of the infant's existence.

Erikson explains that when hope-producing experiences are predominant, the infant matures and is inspired to gradually widen his horizons (e.g., by learning to crawl, a developmental milestone that in turn makes learning to walk a more hopeful possibility). The infant maturing in hope also learns to discern where hopes should be placed and for what he might hope. Erikson notes that this discriminatory process allows the infant to transfer disappointed hopes to better prospects, to dream for the imaginable, and to aspire to what proves possible. In acquiring this capacity for greater discernment and discrimination in his hopes, hopefulness is internalized and becomes intrinsic to his existence, such that when specific hopes go unmet, he does not abandon all hope. In this way, Erikson suggests that hope is not dissimilar to faith; even when rooted in uncertainty and facing catastrophic circumstances, hope can prove itself able to change facts, move mountains, and alter the outcome of events.[28]

Consistent with Erikson's life cycle theory, that positive experiences must outweigh negative ones for healthy development, it is vital that the child have positive early experiences for optimal development of a hopeful attitude. In Erikson's first developmental stage, trust in a care-giving other—generally a single relationship between the infant and primary caregiver—is central to evoking and sustaining hope. However, when trustworthy caregivers are lacking, the infant loses confidence in the world as essentially reliable and has little basis to believe that his desires will be met. Could all hope for a hopeful outlook be lost in infancy?

Donald Capps: Hope, the Reliable Other, and the First Decade of Life

Throughout his forty-year career, Capps has mined the works of Erik Erikson to better equip those in pastoral ministry and care-giving professions.[29] In *Agents of Hope*, Capps again turns to Erikson in an attempt to locate and articulate the genesis of the hopeful self. The fact that Erikson connects hope to trust in a care-giving other is theologically significant to Capps.

Capps finds theological richness in Erikson's claim that at the beginning of one's life, the establishment of hope requires trust in a reliable other or the (divine) "Reliable Other." Predating *Agents of Hope*, Capps's *Deadly Sins and Saving Virtues* also draws on Erikson's life cycle theory. By focusing on Erikson's discussion of the saving virtue of hope, Capps introduces how infant hopes translate into more mature hopes that have theological ends. He suggests that just as hope sustains the infant awaiting the appearance of the care-giving person, it also sustains the "pure in heart" who await the appearance of God: "In both cases, [the hopeful] are sustained by the confidence that, even as they wait, the expected one is preparing to return and, in fact, has a personal need to do so."[30] The expectation that a need will be fulfilled shapes and conditions hope, and is central to both psychological and spiritual development.

In *Agents of Hope*, Capps continues this discussion of how hope matures, explaining how the spirit of hopefulness becomes intrinsically ingrained into one's very being. He states:

As hope matures, an attitude of hopefulness forms that does not depend on the realization of a specific hope because hopefulness is inherently rewarding. Hence, even when some or many of our hopes go unmet, when it would make sense for us to abandon hope, few of us actually do. This is because we have become hopeful selves, and hopefulness has become intrinsic to who we are.[31]

In a more explicitly theological tone, Capps suggests that in the process of spiritual maturation, as in the development of the hopeful self, one develops an intrinsic trust in a divine Reliable Other.

Capps highlights Erikson's first developmental stage, noting that the infant's "general state of trust" indicates that he "has learned to rely on the sameness and continuity of the outer providers."[32] This reliance is a firm conviction that requires little conscious reflection and places unquestioning commitment in the reliability of another.[33] He states that this trust does not depend on another person living up to every expectation and meeting every need but is rather a voluntary act of placing something of value in the hand of another. For Capps, this unquestioning reliance and trust in a caregiving other is commensurate with the trust that the hopeful self endows in God.[34] In Capps's view, God as the Reliable Other emboldens hope and has all power to fuel desires, respond to felt deprivation, and bring about transformation.[35]

In *The Decades of Life: A Guide to Human Development*, Capps reconsiders his understanding of what constitutes the hopeful self. In this work, he expands the possibilities of developing hope later in life by restructuring Erikson's eight developmental stages according to decades. By recasting the life cycle model according to decades, Capps extends the first stage beyond infancy and relocates the conflict of trust versus mistrust in the first nine years of a child's life. From this perspective, in the first decade the child accomplishes feats of discernment that are unimaginable for infants, such as increased attentiveness to trust and trustworthiness in relationships and a heightened cognizance of situations that warrant mistrust.[36] Implicit in Capps's expanded life cycle model is the possibility for children who did not develop a healthy level of trust with their primary caregiver to find trustworthy companions and caregivers elsewhere (i.e., teachers, guidance counselors, ministers, and so on). Capps's decade approach to the developmental stages also has ramifications for the development of the hopeful self.

Though Capps agrees with Erikson that "hope is the earliest and most indispensible virtue for staying alive," he, like Erikson in "Human Strengths and the Cycle of Generations," finds it difficult to identify characteristics of hope in infants.[37] A central dynamic of hope that can be assessed in infants, and in young children for that matter, is mutuality. Erikson suggests that "the infant's smile inspires hope in the adult and, in making him smile, makes him wish to give hope."[38] In this regard, the infant or child can mirror affirmative glances and become an active participant in evoking positive responses that potentially reawaken hope in care-giving others.

Capps's expansion of the first stage of the life cycle is beneficial to care-givers seeking to aid unacknowledged persons who are seemingly devoid of hope. First, children who have missed the opportunity to develop trust in a primary caregiver have additional opportunities to develop hope in communities of support outside of their initial relationships. Second, children, even more so than infants, have the means to awaken hope in others. Later, as we reconsider Capps's understanding of the hopeful self, these two amendments to the genesis of hope will gain greater significance.

When considering Capps's analysis of the origin and maturation of hope, especially its emphasis on trust, I am led to ponder two questions in relation to the stressors faced by Art and Thomas. How can Thomas generate hope in an environment like that of Uth Turn, in which suspicion and mistrust of authority figures and potential foes, and concealment of inner struggles, are not just commonplace but imperative for survival? Similarly, let's examine Art's case. Art's early trust in school was crippled when a once-respected professor denied him the opportunity to share his voice, leading him to ask, "How can I entrust my thoughts to a professor who may or may not hear me?" In both situations, hope for the future is threatened at a level of basic trust. Both young men wonder whether any other person can and will care enough to see their needs and hear their concerns. This, in turn, suggests that fostering hope will require significant work, not only on the part of those lacking a robust capacity to trust, but also on the part of the concerned other who intends to offer them care and support.

At the time of our conversations, Art and Thomas had little "stockpile" of hope in their lives. In Capps's words, they have yet to become "hopeful selves" with "hope intrinsic" to who they are.[39] Could it be possible that for Art and Thomas hope never fully developed? How then might they develop hope in subsequent decades?

Beyond Erikson and Capps: Hope Resurrected

Whether in the first year or the first decade of life, a self grounded in the presence of a responsive care-giving other is central to Erikson's and Capps's understanding of the development of hope. For Capps, this care-giving other—whether an unconditionally loving parent, a teacher, a pastor, or even God as the ultimate Reliable Other—has a central role in conveying hope by mirroring affirmative glances to the deprived self. The hopeful self requires affirmation and mirroring, so that in the eventual absence of the care-giving other, an internalized presence remains. Essential to this paradigm is the need for some care-giving other to see the self, within infancy or the first decade of life, as worthwhile and to hear and respond to her concerns. Beyond mere affirmation, the hopeful self must be *seen* and *heard*.

What, then, of the cut dead reared in a nihilistic culture? What of those who, in the words of the mystical theologian Howard Thurman, are "adrift in the world of men" and who "go nameless up and down the streets of other minds where no salutation greets and no sign is given to mark the place one calls one's own"?[40] Lacking positive recognition and affirmation early in life, how then does the hopeful self fare?

I am reminded of Thomas, who spent much of his childhood and adolescence largely unacknowledged, in correctional facilities, lacking others to see, hear, or respond to his needs. In such an environment, affirmative glances are hard to come by, and the reception of love is minimal beyond the survival-based camaraderie fostered in street gangs. Thomas's identity, it seems, was forged "more by what it lacked than what it possessed."[41] Without sufficient mirroring, this lack, far from constituting his hopeful self, instead readily smothered any sense of hope (if it had developed in any real sense at all), along with his love of self and any love for others. The absence of an affirmative community to present life-giving options, the felt deprivation of decimated employment opportunities, and the impoverished state of his kin fueled within Thomas a flamboyantly wishful, rather than a hopeful, self. The urgent question is: might a hopeful self exist even if hope is not initially implanted by a care-giving other?

In my initial meeting at Uth Turn, one of Thomas's cohorts exclaimed: "I don't trust my momma. Why the f*** should I trust you?" Prolonged reflection on this question has led me to understand that the mistrust exemplified in this young man's interrogation of me extends far beyond his suspicions of my benevolent intentions as a counselor. Capps and Erikson would also recognize the profound truth in this young man's challenge to me. Based on his response of not trusting his "momma," it is probable he would not trust me because he may never have learned as a helpless infant to experience trust in his own mother. It is also possible that this early relationship of mistrust was echoed in the relationship, or lack thereof, with his father. To be sure, these deficiencies reflect the failings of more than his particular parents but those of a whole society. It is likely that his mistrust of me stems from a long pedigree and reflects a painful history of "well-intentioned" authority figures who broke promises, were absent in times of need, and failed to offer mirroring practices that affirm life.

Taking a decades-of-life approach to the life cycle, which posits that young people can develop trust and hope from persons other than their primary caregiver, this young man's lack of trust in his mother does not thwart the possibility of hope's maturation.[42] In Erikson's model, young people who do not receive trust from a primary caregiver find themselves at an impasse as to how they might fill the void left by the lack of an early significant relationship and in turn how to develop the rudiments of hope. However, within Capps's "decades perspective," a community of persons other than the primary caregiver can aid in building trust where mistrust once existed. To this end, a confrontational, but indeed valid, response might be, "You may not trust your mother, but what does that have to do with me? I am not your mother."

Capps's decades perspective, particularly if expanded beyond the first nine years of life, combats firmly rooted mistrust by placing an emphasis on *a community of reliable others*, rather than a singular caregiver, to build rapport and trust and to enliven dormant hope. Implied in the previous statement is the assertion that hope may lie dormant even when not initially implanted by a primary caregiver. That which is seemingly dead is not out of reach of a God who has the power to create life. Thus, through the power of the divine Reliable Other and the assistance of a well-intentioned community of caregivers, hope can be "resurrected." Hope, believed to be cut dead, can emerge and live.

I suggest that hope is intrinsic, something with which we are spiritually endowed, which may lie dormant even without developmental nurturing. Therefore, in the absence of formative seeding there is still a potential for hope. So, if hope perceived to be dead, can, with support, emerge from dormancy and live, it is imperative for caregivers within communities of reliable others to identify the following: the ideal conditions for a seed of hope to flourish and the ecosystemic conditions that can lead to hope's demise. (Find further explanation of the care-giving relationship as an ecosystem in the next chapter). Before we turn to strategies to vitalize hope in chapters 5 and 6, the following section names three threats to hope that can squelch desires for existential change.

Beyond Hopelessness: Internal Threats to Hope

A hopeful attitude involves risks. It also requires effort to maintain in the face of countering forces that, if internalized, sully a hopeful disposition. Capps identifies three primary adversaries to hope that perfectly characterize the struggles faced by the young men presented here—despair, apathy, and shame. He notes that these adversaries of hope are not "absolute evils," in that they counter casual optimism and because the struggle to ward them off creates a more mature understanding of and deeper appreciation for hope.[43] Though these threats to hope possess potentially redemptive qualities, more often they caustically imperil psychological and spiritual health. For greater clarity on how these adversaries—despair, apathy, and shame—affect the cut dead, I offer a descriptive analysis of each of these threats and underscore their ill effects on Art and Thomas.

Threat One: Despair and Its Destructive Derivatives

Capps explains that despair, broadly defined as "suffering without meaning," is chief among the threats to hope. In contrast to those who hope, despairing persons operate from the perception that what is wanted will not happen and that despite intense desires for global change, what is realizable for others is not realizable for them. They may feel as if time is too short to realize a goal or that too much time has been wasted and once-desired long-term goals are unattainable.[44]

Capps says that despair may appear in two forms. The first form is a sense of disgust projected outward and directed toward other persons or institutions.[45] As both Art and Thomas can be said to have qualities comparable to Parenti's category of social dynamite, it is not difficult to frame either of these young men as being highly susceptible to disgust. Thomas, however, particularly exemplifies this derivative of despair because of his consumption-oriented outlook that devalues the lives of others and seeks money and street credibility by any means necessary.

Despite Thomas's efforts to escape the stigma of his street name, Holiday, his history of criminality, his financial obligations to his family, and his dearth of positive support networks made it exceedingly difficult for him to break the cycle of neglect and to envision new possibilities. The viciousness of this cycle, which denied him an opportunity to be seen, to redefine his identity, and to pursue his educational aspirations, perpetuated feelings of despair. This despair was channeled into a "see-me-now" type of posturing, a form of disgust that demanded visibility from other persons and institutions through aggressive verbal threats or physical violence.

The second derivative is depression, an internalized form of despair. Capps explains that depression is caused by a disjunction between one's images of the future and one's ability to make plans of action to bring them about. Thus, the depressed individual is more likely to focus on long-term aspirations and to neglect more realizable short-term goals. Often solid citizens who possess great skill and are loyal in relationships, depressed persons are more prone to hopelessness when loss of a skill or a relationship threatens a long-term goal. The depressed person is thus prone to hopelessness when the desired future hope is jeopardized.[46]

Though Art's outburst of rage on campus is characteristic of disgust, its aftermath of lingering depression was potentially more damaging to this once-hopeful star student. Driven by the consumerist notion of pursuing "A" grades at all costs, Art's self-worth and future were indelibly linked to academic performance. Prior to what he experienced when muted by his professor, Art was a vivacious learner who respected the academic enterprise and scholarly debate, even if he took oppositional stances with his colleagues. As a Princeton student with an exemplary academic record and hopes for doctoral study, he invested much in his critical thinking skills and esteemed the professors who instructed him. However, Art's hope was threatened by the depression that followed in the wake of the traumatic muting incident. He learned that his critical thinking skills were seen as inept and that the loyalty he had invested in his professor did not translate into academic success. With his hope in the future jeopardized by a blemished academic record, Art's zest for scholarship and his once-hopeful disposition were diminished. He became, instead, a withdrawn and depressed classroom seat-filler.

Threat Two: Apathy and the Impact of Acedia and Impulsivity

A second major threat to hope is apathy. Apathy is a state of not caring about what is happening around us, to us, or within us. This threat stands counter to the hoping process that is fueled by desire, because the apathetic person is unaware of having any desires. Capps identifies two derivatives of apathy: acedia and impulsivity.

The acedic person lacks desire because the hoped-for event is so far removed from his daily life that it provides little compelling power to influence him to strive for new possibilities in the present. Capps notes that acedia is a state of not caring and a subsequent "failure to find the world and its activities interesting."[47] In the acedic worldview, in which the object of desire is "lost, absent, difficult to reach, or in the possession of someone else," desire takes the form of a searching susceptible to indifference.[48] Art's self-esteem was shattered in the muting incident. Due to the academic blemish on his transcript, he lacked confidence that his long-term desire for a Ph.D. would ever materialize. A by-product of Art's depression was the characteristic listlessness and lethargy of acedia. With dissipating confidence and threats to a long-held dream, Art grew lethargic and indifferent, and questions of identity and purpose surfaced. The long-armed beast of apathy sideswiped Art's self-esteem.

Another apathetic personality, according to Capps, is what I would call the "present-bound impulsive."[49] Having no apparent realizable hopes, impulsive persons have difficulty seeing beyond the present moment and weighing the consequences of their actions. Lacking in desire and immobilized by repeated and amassed frustrations, the apathetic person finds it difficult to create hopeful future projections. He replaces long-term vision with immediate gratification in the present or near future.[50] With his future stunted, the apathetic person raises the stakes, as he is inclined to stare down undesirable consequences and act anyway. Thomas's alter ego, Holiday, is a prime example of the "present-bound impulsive." Entrenched in a drug culture that fetishizes fanciful objects (such as cars and jewelry) and positioned in a community with few promises for the future, Holiday was consumed by a life of instant gratification, seeking the acquisition of objects to fulfill his wishful fantasies at *any* cost.[51]

Threat Three: Shame and Its Discontents

The third adversary to a hopeful attitude is shame. Shame is a deeply visceral feeling that affects the whole self, which is now seen as defective, soiled, or otherwise diminished. Shame arises from the painful realization that events that were hoped for and confidently expected will not materialize. The shame stems from the realization that one's projected future images were possibly self-illusions or somehow false. This can lead, in turn, to an unwillingness to entertain other hopes.

Capps asserts that individuals with a grandiose or idealistic sense of self are most susceptible to shame experiences. The grandiose person seeks acclaim and recognition, while the idealizing person sets high standards for achievement. The need both to shine and to excel are characteristics inherent in hope, but they also leave the self vulnerable to shame if one fails to receive acclaim or to live up to one's own personal standards. Such shame can lead to the eventual loss of hope.[52]

Both Thomas and Art were hampered by deep shame. Thomas was haunted by his past as Holiday and weighed down by his belief that his current stigma would forever impede his future success and would instead lead to his demise. Art, too, was forced to face some difficult questions of purpose and identity as he endured the shame of receiving a failing grade. This incident forced him to consider whether his hopes for doctoral study were realizable or were instead delusional images. In both cases, shame inflicted a negative blow to the future hopes of these African American young men. Most troubling was that these young men were inhibited from sharing their existential crises because in the cultural malaise of concealment, vulnerability was a risk, and caregivers were viewed suspiciously at best.

As a caregiver, I found it wearying to be under the air of suspicion, constantly trying to chip away at hardened cores of concealment. Living among the cut dead, I often grew nauseated by the putrid smell of dying dreams and withering hopes. In their midst, I was not immune to the cultural contaminants or psychological poisons that threatened their hopes. In fact, after I had gained their trust, as a reliable other, they expected me to internalize their toxic emotions and represent to them more digestible alternatives to their problems.

Capps asserts that in order to offer another person hope, the caregiver must possess some fundament of hope himself. How, then, could I remain hopeful when surrounded by despair? How could I enliven hope in others when I struggled to remain hopeful myself? Why would they be willing to hear my voice when they muted their own, to grant me visibility when they refused to see themselves?

Beyond Toxic Encounters: An Interrupting Hope for Interrupting Caregivers

In May 2008, Alex Kotlowitz's article "Blocking the Transmission of Violence" was the *New York Times Magazine*'s cover story. His detailed ethnographic account followed the violence interrupters as they moved into hotbeds of conflict and defused violent standoffs. At one particularly taxing staff meeting, the interrupters were debriefed about a series of shootings at a local high school and the attack on a former CeaseFire colleague's sons. From Kotlowitz's account, the highly committed violence interrupters appeared "worn down" and "jittery." CeaseFire's founder, Gary Slutkin, noticed the mood in the room and began teaching stress-reduction exercises for the next half-hour. In Kotlowitz's mind, Slutkin somatically communicated, "If they could calm themselves, [then] they could also calm others."[53]

Unfortunately, some caregivers do not have the wherewithal or the external supports to calm themselves or to vitalize their hope during the flash points of disarray. Because of my long treks from Princeton to Newark, I know the emotional weight of bearing others' problems all too well. While the final two chapters of this book propose pragmatic strategies to counter hopelessness for the cut dead, the remainder of this chapter explores the dangers of caring and outlines three allies of hope to help sustain interrupting caregivers. By sharing these care-giving hazards and hope-stimulating allies, I critically analyze how *my own* hope was and continues to be challenged in my role as a caregiver, who also hears and internalizes the stories of muted and invisible persons searching for hope.

On Danger's Edge: Countertransference, Unfiltered Pain, and Triage Care

Caregivers who really care often operate in highly volatile, emotionally charged spaces. Consider that in my experiences with Thomas and Art, layers of mistrust, hypermasculine posturing, and the threat of physical violence compounded feelings of despair, apathy, and shame. For me, the emotional ante was raised to an even higher level, for I know rage personally. I know his name. I have heard his voice in the pit of despair, he has paralyzed me to the point of apathy, and he has masked my face with shame. While I hold him at bay and channel his energies, he is still present within me. Beyond the internal conflicts that have hampered my hope and stifled my self-esteem, like the African American young men in this book, I, too, have lived through the agony of being cut dead. Although surrounded by volatility and wrapped in a fluctuating inner turmoil, as a caregiver, I was challenged to cling to an interrupting hope.

Maintaining my own sanity and clinging to hope amid volatility entailed two central stances. On the one hand, there was a need on my part to process the unfiltered, visceral, and hopeless feelings of young men such as Art and Thomas. On the other hand, I had to be mindful of my own wounds and assess my own emotional investment in feeling unacknowledged. At times when this delicate balance faltered, I found myself highly susceptible to the very hopelessness I was attempting to counter. Psychologists have long referred to the therapist's balancing act as countertransference.

First coined by Freud and later adopted by classical psychoanalysts, the term *countertransference* came to refer to the dynamic process whereby the therapist's own psychological needs and conflicts were evoked by the patient. In the counseling setting, these thoughts and feelings may remain repressed or may be exposed through conscious reactions to patient behavior.[54] As *The Baker Encyclopedia of Psychology and Counseling* notes, countertransference occurs regardless of one's therapeutic approach and can be an excellent instrument for understanding and resolving psychic pain:

> The patient's ability to communicate his or her most painful, disturbing affects and relationships, unconsciously and largely without words, to the therapist, and the therapist's capacity to deeply and unconsciously experience these as his or her own, are profound and might be described as one

of the most truly intimate and spiritual aspects of the therapeutic relationship. To the extent that the patient's pain and needs are traumatic, he or she has not been able to psychically digest or mentalize them so that they cannot be communicated in words. Thus the patient must rely on presenting the analyst with some disturbing emotional experience in order to be understood. This requires the therapist to be aware of the trauma in the counter-transference and at times to stand it and digest it for the patient instead of reacting.[55]

At times the therapist is called upon to internalize the unfiltered pain and trauma of those searching for avenues of hope. Requisite for digesting the internalized trauma of others is a caregiver who is self-critical (able to differentiate the client's issues from her own) and is conscious of self-care (able to manage one's own personal health and hopefulness). When the therapist is less diligent in self-criticism and self-care, *Baker's* explains that the countertransference of processing others' trauma can lead to a neurosis that negatively affects the caregiver:

> This might involve the therapist digesting something that has been indigestible for the patient or detoxifying something that has been too toxic for the patient to allow himself or herself to experience, much less resolve.[56]

Though the experience of digesting and interpreting another's trauma can create a transformative space that brings about the client's healing, ingesting another's toxicity, if the caregiver is not careful, can leave her psychically debilitated and threatened by the client's feelings of hopelessness.

To be sure, offering care to unacknowledged individuals such as Art and Thomas, who carry with them toxic, undigested stories in need of processing, places the caregiver in a psychically dangerous space. In speaking of this danger, a trusted psychologist who for many years counseled similar populations of young men, likened counseling unacknowledged persons to being a triage care physician in the heat of battle.[57] Like the wartime physician and chaplain, the caregiver is forced to internalize the pain, evil, and sorrow of his surroundings, yet remain steadfast and hopeful in his mission to aid those in need.

A creative reading of Capps's *Agents of Hope* has led me to believe that what Capps calls the three allies of hope—trust, patience, and modesty—are tools that can help the triaging caregiver mediate the hope-threatening effects she experiences as countertransference. Capps's three allies correlate with three epiphanies I myself received while working with African American young men who felt muted and invisible. These epiphanies, over time, have become essential to my self-care. On the surface, these epiphanies may appear to be somewhat cliché, but they were born out of personal pain, clinical practice, theological contemplation, hours of therapy, and sustained reflection on Capps's three allies of hope. I consider these allies and my epiphanies alongside one another as tactics to assist caregivers in managing internal stress and maintaining hope while working with persons who feel muted and invisible.

Ally One: Trust in the Changer

For those who have been previously unacknowledged, trust is not freely given but must be earned repeatedly. This is underscored by the question that I was confronted with on my first night at Uth Turn: "I don't trust my momma, why the f*** should I trust you?" Though this challenging question typifies the contested space in which I operated at Uth Turn, some other African American young men with whom I have spoken were equally reluctant to trust. This is evident in the decline of Art, who after the traumatic muting incident ceased to trust colleagues and professors with his thoughts in classroom debate for fear of being further silenced. Thus, the caregiver has a daunting task of building rapport in a culture of mistrust and concealment in which the clients are reluctant to engage in critical introspection.

Caregivers need enough energy to build the trust of these young men, and they incur a certain amount of stress from the pressures of time in which one must effect change. In both Art's and Thomas's cases, there was a limited window of time to establish rapport and work toward a more hopeful end. Art's situation involved a crisis intervention, and though edgy at the time of our meeting, he would soon have to reenter the institution at which his explosive reaction occurred. Thomas and his cohorts at Uth Turn were involved in a juvenile reentry program, through which they would be released back into the community. This left me, as their counselor, with only five to six one-hour sessions in which to attempt to provide tools that might foster hope and prevent further criminality. Both situations afforded me, as their counselor, only a small amount of time to assist those in need.

Considering the ethos of mistrust, the magnitude of the problems, and the limited window of time to effect change, some caregivers would view the situations facing Art and Thomas as seemingly hopeless and would work with them under such a premise. Other more hopeful caregivers, myself included, might thrust themselves into these difficult situations and, despite the stress and pressure involved, seek to bring about change in the lives of those in need. Though the latter response seems more appropriate and valiant, I would come to learn that it can be as harmful to the client as the former approach.

By fully investing oneself in a pressure-filled situation to alter the client's thoughts and actions, the caregiver places considerable trust in himself and his own abilities to change the life of another. Under this rubric, the caregiver takes on the lion's share of responsibility for the success or failure of the client. Such thinking sets up the caregiver for hopelessness and despair, increasing his susceptibility to extreme disgust or depression when the intended receiver of one's care does not "change" at the rate one had anticipated.

As a caregiver, I was also influenced and burdened by a culture of over-achievement. I sought to work with the clients with the most severe problems, and I pursued change at all costs, even to the detriment of my physical and emotional health. As a pastoral counselor at Uth Turn, and one who worked with African American students in the Princeton community, I fully invested myself in the lives of numerous young people and often came to feel personally responsible for their success or failure. Though many of them exceeded my expectations, I focused greater attention on those who did not fare so well. I harbored disgust at those who neared their goal only to sabotage their success with poor decision-making. Likewise, I sometimes grew depressed at not being able to do more for those in situations in which they had little power over their body or voice. For months, I found myself consumed with the problems of those I sought to help and, at times, incapable of aiding those in, what I perceived as, their need to search for hope.

I eventually altered my point of view on effecting change in counseling after receiving a revelation, ironically, while teaching a workshop to social workers on self-care. We agreed on the fact that, as caregivers, we were expected to face grave interpersonal and social difficulties but also to extract hopeful elements from people's stories. I then suggested that we alter how we interpret those stories by viewing ourselves as "(change) agents of hope."

To explain this alternative view of the caregiver's unique approach to hope and change, I likened our work to that of travel agents who book airline tickets, reserve rental cars, and secure hotel arrangements. What the travel agent does *not* do, however, is fly the plane, drive the car, or check the traveler into the hotel. The agent mediates travel, but only many others (including God) can ensure that the traveler arrives safely. Similarly, as change agents, caregivers mediate change, but only God, the Divine Changer, can change hearts and minds such that the troubled person can alter his or her situation.

This epiphany led me to understand that though mistrust may dominate the thinking of unacknowledged young men, for the caregiver, trust in the Reliable Other (God) and reliable others (i.e., communities of support such as trained mental health professionals) is essential. Recall that Capps suggests that trust is the necessary condition for hope.[58] Trust points beyond the immediate situation, enables the caregiver to risk herself to an uncertain future, and destabilizes despair.[59]

For caregivers, the ability to entrust the toxic feelings evoked from internalizing others' stories to the Reliable Other or reliable others is not only invaluable but also imperative for psychic and spiritual health. Though the caregiver must maintain confidences, he must also rely on processing stories with professionally trained reliable others (and perhaps clinical supervisors) to help interrupt feelings of countertransference that may imperil the caregiver's own sense of hope. This is professionally responsible and necessary for self-care. For persons of faith, entrusting feelings to God provides another avenue to eliminate psychic toxins. In addition to being a place of release, a trusted relationship with the Reliable Other becomes a source of replenishment where one can gain a hopeful perspective.

Entrusting God with the care of those I sought to help combated my thoughts of disgust and depression and challenged my cynicism that after the client left my care, things would potentially fall apart and nothing could be done to make it right.[60] The act of trusting God generated more hope in the present moment that my human action was aided by divine intervention and that pockets of resistance could emerge at any given moment. This trust in the Reliable Other further helped me see that my limited efforts to effect change were always aided by divine power. By knowing that I had a place to release my emotional toxins and having the assurance that I was not the primary or sole agent of change, I acquired more courage and hope to risk my psychic health to help embattled others.

Ally Two: Be Patient in Planting Seeds

If one cannot always control one's ability to change others, neither can one control the timetable by which they choose to change. The second ally that sustains the caregiver's hope is *patience*. According to Capps, patience keeps hopes alive by providing the necessary endurance and perseverance to wait for an anticipated outcome.[61] However, for persons conditioned to help the suffering—particularly codependent caregivers who attach their self-worth to serving others—being patient is difficult. My work with the unacknowledged has taught me that patience is a hopeful act that differs from inactivity and interrupts self-righteous desires to care.

It cannot be overlooked that, at times, in my work with cut-dead African American young men, I was stricken by codependency. A counselor I was seeing emphasized that working with unacknowledged African American young men stressed me because of my high degree of personal investment in their lives. As their caregiver, I found it difficult not to envision the young men in front of me as relatives and friends who had lost their way. Art represented one end of this spectrum for me—a gifted young man who defied public stigma by excelling academically and staying out of trouble only to have his hopes dashed as he neared the height of his dreams. On the other end of this personal spectrum was Thomas, who, through lack of resources and poor decision-making, clamored for hope and life in an environment that expected him to spend time in jail, pull a trigger, or die on the wrong end of a gun.

As a minister, counselor, relative, and friend, I have seen young men in both situations—ones at the height of success and just starting to change, and others broken by dashed hopes and plummeting into apathy. For example, in my thirteen months at Uth Turn, less than ten of the nearly two hundred young men I worked with did *not* return to criminal behavior, get severely injured, or even get killed after leaving the program. One of the program's most promising students robbed a bank the day after his release. I have also witnessed students at Princeton, like Art, lose their vigor for achieving academic excellence after enduring traumatic incidents. Recognizing the dire nature and urgency of the situation, my natural inclination was to rush to the aid of those seeking help and to urge them to see life differently sooner rather than later. My tendencies toward haste in helping, however, would eventually threaten my hope.

Capps writes that "impatience—the desire to force events to occur before their appointed time—is the very hallmark of our time."[62] This impatience is often created by a restless sense that if change does not happen immediately, it may never happen. However, as I emphasized in the previous section, actually changing the action of the individual seeking care is beyond the reach of the caregiver. Still, the inability to make a person change remains frustrating. Equally frustrating and discouraging for caregivers working with at-risk populations is the lack of seeing immediate positive results from one's efforts. Nonetheless, I would soon understand why Capps believes that "patience is the assurance that the hoped-for outcome is worth the frustration."[63]

Early in my work at Uth Turn, the frustration of not seeing clients make significant change after our work together made it increasingly difficult for me to function on my job. Then, one of my first clients made a statement that altered how I view success in counseling and made me understand the necessity for patience. On average, my weekly client load was five or six one-hour, one-on-one sessions with select clients at Uth Turn. Generally, it took two to three of those sessions to begin to develop trust and rapport. In the fifth and final session with one particular client, I was told, "Mr. Greg, I appreciate everything you've taught me and helped me think about over the past five weeks. I'll never forget it. But, I still got some more hustlin' in me." This was possibly one of the most honest statements that I received from a client at Uth Turn. Sustained reflection on this statement with another mental health professional helped me revise my understanding of patience and alter how I did my work there. The epiphany that followed proved formative in shaping how I viewed my role as caregiver and maintained hope in other short-term counseling situations.

What I gathered from my client's statement was that the caregiver, as teacher, guide, and advocate, has a responsibility "to plant seeds of hope." These seeds may take weeks, months, or years to take root, if at all, and it is likely that the caregiver will not be around to watch the seeds blossom. This epiphany was liberating for me, as I realized that the act of planting seeds is not a passive resignation to accept whatever happens but an active patience that endures in spite of knowing one may never see the desired fruits of change. Resisting frustration and hopelessness in the absence of seeing desired changes requires an act of reframing, grounded in trusting that the Reliable Other is working on the sufferer's behalf.

Ally Three: Engage in Modest but Respectful Fearless Dialogue

Capps contends that *modesty* staves off shame and helps put hopes in perspective.[64] For Capps, a modest attitude helps a person avoid becoming overwhelmed by failure. This modest attitude enables one to retain hope in difficult situations because modesty minimizes self-deception, helps one remain situated within problems of the real world, and teaches respect for other people and the vast power of the universe. Capps further asserts that a modest attitude enables one to "remain part of the scheme of things and not attempt to stand outside of reality itself; [hopeful persons] have 'a degree of modesty vis-à-vis the power and workings of the nature of the cosmos' and 'some feeling of commonality, if not communion, with other people.'"[65] Having the attitude of the modest caregiver who does not flee reality, is self-critical, and is respectfully in communion with other people and the universe is vital for caregivers forced to navigate issues of critical distance in serving the unacknowledged.

Perhaps most threatening to my own sense of hope was the stress I incurred in navigating the gulf of critical distance between myself and my unacknowledged clients. I would soon learn that a modest attitude and respectful confrontation were essential for interrupting the real, and at times superficial, differences that prevented fearless dialogue.

At the beginning of this chapter, I intentionally avoided mentioning that the first class I led at Uth Turn, the day I met Thomas, was on many accounts a teaching failure. Though all the right components for generating fearless dialogue seemed to be present—rap music, a captivating subject, and a personal story—the students sensed that something about me was disingenuous. They were correct. Despite the music, subject matter, and my personal story, I was a foreigner to them, given my dress, background, and the way I spoke. Furthermore, my motivations were misguided. Reflection on that class led me to the epiphany that I, too, was immodestly posturing, presenting to them only the small part of my personal story that I thought would gain me credibility and acceptance. By not being forthright and sharing myself more honestly with them, their suspicions were heightened and my credibility was called into question even more. I learned from that point forward that, in their individual and collective company, I had to be as honest as I could and respectfully insist they do the same.

As Capps notes, the modest person does not flee reality or deceive himself but faces the pain of this world. As a caregiver, I came to recognize that in order to promote change, I had to take a chance and risk being vulnerable and transparent. When speaking with Art, Thomas, and other unacknowledged young men, I learned that, in the contested space of sharing painful truth, both parties have something to hide and something to lose and therefore must actively choose to be forthright. Particularly, considering our limited time and the magnitude of problems facing these young men, kind platitudes and empathetic leading were ineffective.

Thomas and Art helped me realize the importance of insisting on truthful and fearless dialogue. Thomas shared with me that, as a result of being in the correctional system, he and other members of Uth Turn learned to "throw batteries," that is, to manipulate the system by evading the truth and saying what counselors and authority figures wanted to hear so they could achieve their desired ends. The young men's manipulative tactics speak to how savvy clients exploit even well-intentioned caregivers. Likewise, Art expressed disinterest in counseling because a previous therapist sat at a physical and intellectual distance and never challenged his positions. As a counselor, viewed initially as "worlds apart" from those I sought to help, I could only demand honesty if I faced my own fears and modeled honest, direct, fearless dialogue.

Like tightrope walking, modestly confrontational dialogue requires great balance and bold acceptance of risks. This type of dialogue is potentially harmful to the caregiver's hopes because he must learn to claim and use past failures, fears, and inadequacies as tools for interrupting despair, apathy, and shame and as instruments to build hope. In this process, the caregiver walks the thin line of sharing too little and not creating the necessary relationship for dialogue, and sharing too much and shifting the focus of the counseling session toward the counselor. At the same time, the counselor must employ a directness that challenges his falsehood and identifies and evades "batteries" of manipulation. Therefore, in fearless dialogue, the caregiver must balance the nurture and admonition of others with strategic self-disclosure and heightened self-awareness. A respectfully confrontational atmosphere that presses both counselor and counselee to face problems, grapple with psychosocial pressures, and set obtainable goals is emotionally intense and draining for the caregiver. It often took me two days to recover from three hours of counseling at Uth Turn and months of therapy to process the countertransference evoked in those fearless dialogues.

***

Capps suggests that the three allies of hope—trust, patience, and modesty—are mutually supportive, for as we trust, we are able to exercise greater patience, and in modesty we are conscious of the necessity of trust.[66] Further reflection on the intersection of these allies reminds me that I, too, have been previously unacknowledged and must figuratively and literally sit in the counselee's seat to heal and retain hope. I must entrust my pain to reliable others and the Reliable Other. I must be patient and know that my "words taken for granted are already planted"[67] and the seeds of healing that others sow in me will take root. Finally, I must not evade the uncomfortable and often unsettling challenges directed toward me by modest, respectfully confrontational caregivers. From this purview, as a counselee and counselor, I stand amongst the wreckage of dashed dreams and normalized chaos. Transfixed with awe and the horror of the sheer destruction I see, I gain a fuller understanding of the sacrifice and heart it takes for young men to clamor for hope in the face of imminent death.

A Final Word: Stillbirth

Elisha, my first son, never breathed his first breath. Yet, my two living children call his name in remembrance every night in prayer. They see their older brother as a guardian angel and reliable other who gives them courage to hope for better days. Their bedtime prayers interrupt my belief that death has the final answer. Hope, believed to be cut dead, can emerge and live. But since the seed of hope in the cut dead may be nearly imperceptible, caregivers must possess heightened awareness to see this miracle of life cloaked by the shadow of death.

Fit to Survive

Two guns in my back, yet I choose to fight

These are situations that infuse the night

Face pressed on a fence, yet I'm not tense

We only value heaven, if we see the hell
around it

And value situations if we live to tell about it

—William K. Gravely

CHAPTER FIVE

THE DEATH OF MEANINGFUL EXISTENCE AND THE BIRTH OF MIRACULOUS SOLUTIONS

On a sniffly winter day, surrounded by soiled tissues, I peered out a frosted window and above the fence line to take notice of dozens of needleless pines and leafless oaks. From the vantage point of my bedroom window, with eyes unclouded by DayQuil, I could see through a clearing, deep into the forest. Not an outdoorsman, I had yet to brave the elements to see what lay beyond the wooded stockade, but Mother Nature was giving me a gift. For just a moment, on that unusually cold Georgia day, I could see deep into the woods, beyond the trees. In a matter of weeks, spring would blossom, the pines would send forth needles, the oaks would grow leaves, and the heart of the forest would again be a mystery.

A skilled hunter once told me that in dense forests, even the smallest clearing provides a unique vantage point to zero in on the target. At first glance, the hardened exteriors of African American young men who are cut dead but still alive may appear as impenetrable woodlands. However, on occasion, exceptional clearings of hope arise in seemingly mundane moments of conversation. In these fleeting moments, perceptive caregivers, with eyes unclouded by prejudgment, are given the opportunity to see deep into the hearts of the unacknowledged and to zero in on seeds of hope. In order to seize the gift, in these fleeting moments, the caregiver must be equipped to maneuver through briary language traps, see beyond a dense stockade of ~~problems~~, and reframe time in order to enliven hopeful possibilities. Stephen and Carl are two such young men, who, in needleless moments, offered clearings to their hearts. Meet Stephen:

> My size-thirteen shoes hung slightly over the edge of the bridge. I peered down 45 feet and could see the traffic racing beneath me. The blood ran cold in my veins. I closed my eyes and all I could think of was, "If I kill myself nobody will have to worry about me. It will be so much easier." So I took one big step . . . A few weeks later I woke up from a coma. They said it was *miracle* that I lived.

Within the sterile walls of the county jail's psychiatric facility, twenty-year-old Stephen and I reflected on his failed suicide attempt. Two years had passed since this high-school basketball phenomenon had nearly plunged to his death and had been in a coma for weeks. His wiry six-foot-four-inch frame still ached daily from the effects of the fall. Though he still suffered from severe seizures and headaches, his brokenness was most evident in his words. He divulged how he felt shattered emotionally by careless parents who abandoned him at birth and frustrated by his loving adoptive parents' naïveté concerning his pain. He anguished at feeling alone in the limelight, torn between two worlds, in one a "popular" star basketball player and in another a person with no true friends. Haunted by a life of petty crimes, sexual promiscuity, and drug addiction, he now sought to come to grips with how he could become a more faithful Christian. In utter dismay, he explained his suicide attempt and errant life choices in one sentence, "They didn't know me, and I didn't know myself."

The pain and confusion of being misunderstood, unacknowledged, and not fully "known" that led Stephen to step off a bridge parallels the mixed emotions of Carl, a bright, seemingly gregarious high-school student who prided himself on academic excellence and perfect school attendance yet also tried to take his own life. The day after his suicide attempt, Carl put on what he called his "happy face,"[1] went to school, and fortuitously met Insoo Kim Berg, a master clinician and cocreator of Solution-Focused Brief Therapy. Berg was preparing for a lecture at Carl's school when he approached her and spoke a few words in Japanese. He politely assisted her with her belongings and helped her get settled for her presentation. Then with a straight face, Carl blurted out to Berg that he had tried to kill himself the previous night. Following this confession, he showed her a "superficial scar" on his neck where he had attempted to slit his throat.

Shortly after Berg completed her lecture, she had a therapeutic conversation with this troubled young man who was in search of the "real Carl." Fully transcribed in Steve de Shazer's *More Than Miracles: The State of the Art of Solution-Focused Brief Therapy,* Carl describes in his interviews with Berg his close encounter with death:

> I tried to go to sleep, but my brother, he keeps bothering me. . . . I was like, no, I need to go to sleep; I need to go to school in the morning. . . . So I got up; I knocked on my mom's door, and I told her, I said, "Can you please put the CD player in his room so he can stop bothering me?" So he started using profanity at me or whatever. And then I used it back, a lot. And then I tried to calm myself down by going outside and trying to walk. . . . I caught the bus to my aunt's house. Aunt Jasper. And while I was walking over there, I feel like this dark cloud over my head, and it was pitiful. Everything from love, hate, anger, frustration just collided. And when I went in there, I went in the kitchen. I rinsed off the knife, a big knife. And, luckily it wasn't sharp enough 'cause I held my head back while my aunt was right there. She was, you know, intoxicated, but she wasn't paying me any mind or anything. And I leaned my head back. . . . And then I just started cutting.[2]

For both Stephen and Carl, maintaining a disingenuous persona eventually became so overwhelming that they could not conceive of continuing life as they knew it. But as Stephen noted, a miracle happened, and they "lived to tell about it." Faced with putting the pieces of their lives back together, they sat before caregivers who approached the art of hearing stories differently than many of their peers.

Surviving a suicide attempt was indeed miraculous for Stephen and Carl, but survival had its own complications. Hopes were still deadened, and these young men still felt their lives had little worth. But in the company of an attentive caregiver, they told their stories, searching for ways to piece their shattered lives back together. Oddly, seemingly imperceptible miracles burst forth in these fearless dialogues that transformed how these young men viewed themselves and the world around them. This chapter critically analyzes the philosophy, history, and practice of Solution-Focused Brief Therapy—an unconventional therapeutic approach to hearing and interpreting lived stories that creates spaces for miracles to emerge.

Solution-Focused Brief Therapy (SFBT) is a future-oriented, strength-based, goal-directed therapeutic approach that shifts the focus of treatment from past problems to future solutions. Developed by Steve de Shazer and his colleagues at the Brief Family Therapy Center, this approach "draws upon clients' strengths and resiliencies by focusing on their own previous or conceptualized solutions and exceptions to their problems. . . . [T]hen through a series of interventions, [therapists encourage] clients to do more of those behaviors."[3] This frame of thinking is radically different from traditional models of therapy that focus on uncovering and resolving past difficulties.

This chapter unfolds with a brief description of the evolution of SFBT and its departure from more traditional conceptions of therapy. Following this is an analysis of how solution-focused therapists conceptualize language, build rapport, and create safe spaces for change. The chapter concludes with an exploration of solution-focused techniques that counter the ills of despair, apathy, and shame. Throughout the chapter, I return to Stephen's and Carl's cases for further analysis. However, to establish the need for miracle-producing conversation, I will first shed light on how the shadow of death attacks the meaningful existence of African American young men.

A Loss of Meaningful Existence and the Shadow of Death

In a gang-ridden community in which gunplay is recreational and pistol smoke rises in billows, Rev. Toby Sanders, pastor and founder of Beloved Community Church, stood in a dimly lit sanctuary and preached a bone-chilling sermon on the "valley of the shadow of death." Before congregants accustomed to attending the funerals of African American young men slain in urban warfare, Sanders evoked the image of the "valley" as a military post. Flanked by two mountains, the valley was a place of combat where rival factions met to wage war. Before battle, the opposing forces faced each other from adjacent mountains, the white gleam of the morning sun reflecting upon their backs and casting shadows of the battle to come in the cavernous valley. The shadows in the valley were an ever-present reminder of lurking death.

Sanders then unpacked the allusively rich and poetic phrasing of the "shadow of death." Deconstructing the Hebrew word *tsalmoevath*, Sanders illustrated the close relationship between the words *tsal* ("shadow" and "darkness") and *tsalem* ("image" and "empty shadow"). Through this connection, Sanders asserted that the shadow of death was a dual image, of the fearsome world around us and of that which we fear most in ourselves, a lack of meaning and worth. The shadow was deeply threatening because the root of all fear is death.

Stephen and Carl narrowly escaped the grave, and plodding through the valley, they lived to tell their stories. Yet, the ghostly shadow of death haunted their daily living and possessed their outlook on life. If one is not careful, the shadow of death can dim even the most glaring and hopeful spirit, particularly for African American men, in whom reminders of mortality are present from their first breath to their last. The facts and figures below, which show the fragility of life for African American men from womb to tomb, are heart-stopping.

Statistics reveal that African American children are challenged by the threat of death moments after their first breath. In 2009, the average infant mortality rate for American-born children was 6.39 infant deaths per 1,000 live births.[4] White infants fell below the national average at 5.3 infant deaths per 1,000 live births. Grimly, the infant mortality rate for black infants that year was 12.64 deaths per 1,000 live births. The mortality rate for black infants was 2.38 times the rate for white infants.[5]

The numbers are more staggering in the teenage years. In a 2010 report from the Centers for Disease Control and Prevention (CDC) entitled "Mortality among Teenagers Aged 12-19 Years: United States, 1999–2006," Arialdi Miniño argued that teenage mortality was a public health issue because the majority of the deaths were caused by external injuries such as accidents, homicide, and suicide, all of which, by definition, are preventable. The shadows of "preventable deaths" loom heavily over growing black male bodies. The data reveals the death rate for non-Hispanic white teenagers during this period was 47.0 deaths per 100,000 people compared with 47.1 for Hispanic and 64.5 for black teenagers. Among male and female teenagers, non-Hispanic black males have the highest death rate of 94.1 deaths per 100,000 people. In this cohort, "the risk of dying from homicide among non-Hispanic black male teenagers (39.2 per 100,000 population) is more than twice that of Hispanic males (17.1 per 100,000 population) and about fifteen times that of non-Hispanic white males (2.6 per 100,000)."[6] Another CDC study in 2007 substantiated these results and found that homicide accounted for 51 percent of the deaths of black males between the ages of fifteen and twenty-four. Two other preventable causes followed: accidents (22.9 percent) and suicide (6 percent).[7]

Life expectancy studies even show that the death bell tolls earlier for black men than for other demographic groups. The year 2007 marked record highs in American life expectancy, with the average reaching 77.9 years for all Americans. These record highs were also notable for white females (80.7 years), black females (77.0 years), white males (75.8 years), and black males (70.2 years). The year 2007 was the first recorded year that life expectancy for black males exceeded seventy years.[8]

Statistics show that from cradle to grave, even on the sunniest of days, the shadow of death sweeps behind African American men, reminding them that life is fragile. Whether these sightings of the shadow of death come from watching parents grieve their murdered teenage son on the news or from attending the funeral of a friend who stepped off a bridge, the shadow's presence is felt. The death shadow also descends when African American young men are cut dead in social interaction. These constant reminders weigh heavy on the soul and alert the cut dead of their fragile and temporary existence and its lack of meaning and worth. Being passed over is a social death that leads the cut dead to reckon with the existential angst of what it would be like if they were dead. Would anyone notice? Would anyone care?

Social psychologists have indicated that humans have an innate need to maintain a belief in a meaningful existence and to avoid thoughts of death.[9] For young men such as Stephen, Carl, and William Gravely, finding clearings of light in a shadow-cast world is a life-or-death endeavor. Few caregivers think of their work with such urgency, but in light of the preceding statistics, the clock is ticking for the cut dead. By giving voice and visibility to the cut dead and generating swift and effective results to seemingly intractable problems, SFBT is sensitive to the fleeting moment.

History: Beyond the Living Room— The Historic Evolution of SFBT

In the mid-twentieth century, groups of classically trained therapists grew frustrated with the uncertainty of their methods, the length of treatment, and the paucity of their results. In this same era, "gimmicky" interventions were emerging that produced unexplainable and unexpected success. This section explores two therapeutic camps that developed alternative methods of structural approaches to change and became predecessors of SFBT. The first camp actually consisted of an individual, named Milton Erickson, whose magical therapeutic style left clients spellbound and readied for change. The second camp consisted of members of the Mental Research Institute in Palo Alto, California (The Palo Alto Group), who pioneered a therapeutic approach using language-bending and paradoxical change. Both camps of unconventional theory-practitioners were formative in the development of SFBT.

Milton Erickson

Erickson, an eccentric psychiatrist, utilized a combination of hypnosis and storytelling to reframe time and generate within his clients an expectation of change.[10] Holding to the enduring beliefs that "change was not only possible but inevitable"[11] and that "only a small change is necessary to initiate change in a system,"[12] Erickson's therapeutic approach focused on the patient's present actions and future goals, rather than on some past event.

The Palo Alto Group

From extensive research in human communications and therapeutic practice, therapists at the Mental Research Institute in Palo Alto systematically expanded Erickson's work on change. The Palo Alto Group believed that people come to therapy equipped with knowledge that can solve their situation, but they are discouraged from resolving the problem because of numerous failed attempts. One therapeutic technique the group employed to bolster change was "reframing." Reframing means to "change the conceptual and/or emotional setting or viewpoint in relation to how a situation is experienced and to place it in another frame which fits the 'facts' of the same concrete situation equally well or even better, and thereby changing its entire meaning."[13] Key to reframing is the ability of the client to see the situation differently. Although the facts of the situation remain the same, the therapist helps the client see the facts from a different angle.

Another therapeutic technique was the introduction of paradox. One example of paradox employed by the Palo Alto Group utilizes techniques of "advertising" instead of concealing. In dealing with the cases of Stephen and Carl, who had gone to great lengths to conceal their authentic selves from others, the Palo Alto Group might encourage the young men to advertise the very thing they most want to conceal. In Stephen's case, this might involve confessing that, though he appreciates his adoptive parents, he longs to meet his biological ones. In Carl's case, this might entail not smiling and putting on a "happy face" when he is unhappy but, instead, telling others overtly that he is displeased. For the Palo Alto Group, this is the technique of choice when concealment is the client's attempted solution. The group reasons that "even when the subject cannot bring himself to carry out instruction, the mere fact that it is on his mind, that he now sees a potential way out [or a *clearing*], may be enough to change his behavior."[14]

The Brief Family Therapy Center

While Erickson's hypnotherapeutic storytelling provided inroads to untangling seemingly intractable problems, and the Palo Alto Group's paradoxical resolutions provided avenues to unsnarl gridlocked problems, Steve de Shazer came to realize, from his own therapeutic encounters, that a problem's solution, not its cause, was the most important thing in therapy. This led him to conclude that even when the causes of problems appear complex, often the solution is not.

With this hunch about the nature of solution-based thinking, in 1969, de Shazer began developing a brief therapy model of his own, which emphasized the importance of solutions rather than focusing on the causes of problems.[15] Nine years later, along with his wife, Insoo Kim Berg, and a few colleagues, de Shazer founded the Brief Family Therapy Center, a not-for-profit training and research institution and outpatient mental health clinic that served a racially, ethnically, and socioeconomically diverse pool of clients in Milwaukee, Wisconsin.[16] Three decades after its development, SFBT has been used by counselors, educators, and social workers around the world to assist individuals, married couples and families, substance abusers, and schizophrenics.[17] Given its widespread appeal and effectiveness with diverse populations, it has surprisingly modest origins.

In spite of the psychological theory and philosophical constructs that structure SFBT, the practice of this model developed organically from trial and error. In fact, research shows that Steve de Shazer and Insoo Kim Berg first interviewed clients in their living room while a team of therapists listened to the therapeutic conversation from the stairs. Once they reached a stopping point, the team then moved to the kitchen to discuss the case.[18] Eve Lipchik, one of the founding members of the Brief Family Therapy Center, recounts that even the shift from problem-focused brief therapy to SFBT was a random occurrence.

In her book *Beyond Techniques in Solution-Focused Therapy*, Lipchik reports that near the end of a third counseling session, after seeing no results in the case of a family with a rebellious teenager, a member of the team of therapists, observing the session from behind a one-way mirror, said, "Why don't we ask them to make a list of what they don't want to change for next time?" This question was an intriguing way of asking the family what indeed was good in their household. Sometime later, the family members not only returned with sizable lists of what they appreciated about one another but also reported less tension in their home.[19] Based on these positive results, the therapists came to develop more future-oriented, solution-focused questions. Four years into their work together, the Milwaukee-based team coined the term "Solution-Focused Brief Therapy" after discovering that finding "exceptions to the problem" aided in finding lasting solutions.[20]

A therapeutic focus on exceptions seeks to modify the client's perception of the complaint. Exceptions are when one might expect a problem to occur but it didn't.[21] Exceptions contrast with the complaint and open potential avenues for attaining solutions if amplified by the therapist or the client.[22] Solution-focused brief therapists believe that concentrating on exceptions, as opposed to problems is more effective.[23]

The search for exceptions was one of the major innovations that separated the Brief Family Therapy Center from Milton Erickson and the Palo Alto Group. Exceptions suggest that therapists do not even need to know what the problem is, as long as they and the client have set an attainable goal. The search for exceptions stands in stark contrast to many therapeutic approaches, which seek to uncover the root of pain by delving into the client's past or unconscious. De Shazer and his colleagues distanced themselves even from Erickson and the Palo Alto Group, who focused on reframing the present problem. Solution-focused brief therapists believed that clients defined their present problems in such rigid forms that future change appeared unlikely. For example, though a couple may state they are always fighting, de Shazer believed that if the therapist asks the right questions, the couple would find out that there are times when they do get along, even if only for a couple of minutes each day. In search of exceptions, de Shazer once asked an embattled couple if they fought while brushing their teeth that morning. Similarly, given our present focus on unacknowledged African American men, we might find that these young people are not muted and invisible at all times or in every relationship. From this point of view, the "problem" is not wholly confounding. The challenge, then, is for the caregiver to find exceptional clearings to help the client begin to see previously unrecognized opportunities for a different future.

Thus, for de Shazer, solving problems involves doing or seeing something differently. Achieving this goal of seeing and acting differently requires the therapist to create a safe space for the client to begin envisioning new possibilities and to imagine a solution. To create avenues for constructive dialogue, de Shazer believes therapists must exercise caution in their speech, and steer clear of the dark clouds of problem-talk.

Philosophy: Beyond Dark Clouds— Constructivist Philosophy and SFBT

The philosophy behind solution-focused techniques detours from the therapeutic approaches of Freud, Salvador Minuchin, Selvini Palazzoli, and others who attend mainly to past behaviors or look behind or beneath the client's comments or gestures to discover hidden meanings. This detour from a focus on the past is demonstrated in Carl's case when his solution-focused therapist, Insoo Kim Berg, moved beyond problem discovery and problem explanation. The therapist instead seeks to facilitate recognition of new possibilities for viewing the situation. Consider the following therapeutic response to Carl's mention of a "dark cloud."

In recounting the night of his suicide attempt, Carl disclosed to Berg that when walking to his Aunt Jasper's house, he felt a "dark cloud" over his head in which "everything from love, hate, anger, [and] frustration just collided."[24] Some therapists would immediately follow Carl's reference to the "dark cloud" as a signal of repressed emotions that need addressing. But Berg circumvented the "dark cloud" of Carl's past. Instead, she opted for a more hopeful, future-oriented approach and "join[s] around [his] competence [to] establish some examples of his competence and history of ability to make good decisions for himself."[25] The approach of highlighting present competencies to *construct* future good decisions represents a significant shift from traditional *structural* psychotherapeutic styles. I further define the philosophies behind these variant therapeutic approaches below in order to distinguish the uniqueness of SFBT and to highlight why constructing new future possibilities is central to this work.

Structural Approaches to Care

Although structuralism encompasses a complex array of theories utilized in many disciplines, in this context, structuralism is defined as "a movement for determining and analyzing the basic, relatively stable elements of a system."[26] This movement seeks to uncover the meaning of a sign, behavior, or word from exploration of a deeper underlying structure. Generally, claiming a stance of scientific objectivity, structuralists use detailed observational analysis of speech, gestures, or behaviors to reveal hidden truths. De Shazer notes that traditional forms of psychotherapy, including brief psychodynamic therapy and most family therapy, assert that "before a problem can be solved or an illness or disease cured, it is necessary to find out what is wrong to make a diagnosis."[27] Hence, they share the structuralist's assumption that "rigorous analysis of the problem leads to understanding it and its underlying causation or disease; *what the client presents or complains about is ordinarily seen as just a symptom of something else.*"[28] As the previous quote suggests, many structuralist thinkers believe that symptoms are by-products of some underlying problem. Thus, if the underlying problem is corrected, the symptoms will disappear.

Using this cause-and-effect line of thinking, a structural therapist might ask Carl about his stormy collision of love, anger, hate, and frustration and then proceed to search for underlying causes of these feelings. To this end, structural therapists have the goal of breaking up "problem-maintaining mechanisms" that exist on various causative levels. This approach often requires long-term therapeutic assistance in order to unearth and heal deep-seated pathologies that lie in the client's individual and/or systemic history.[29]

Constructivist Approaches to Care

Therapists who utilize constructivist philosophy or post-structural thought approach problems, symptoms, and client complaints in a manner different from that of structural thinkers. Derived from literary studies, "constructivism" is "used as a label for a point of view, a way of looking at, thinking of, and talking about reality, in other words, epistemology. Reality, or better realities, are invented rather than discovered; humans build the worlds in which they live."[30] Operating under the premise of inventing versus discovering realities in the human condition, constructivists or post-structural thinkers doubt that meaning is stable and attainable through transformation. On the contrary, they believe that meaning is open to view and can be known through social interaction and negotiation.[31]

In both thought and practice, constructivist brief therapy is exploratory by nature. To conduct this exploratory mode of therapy, both briefly and effectively, constructivists seek to "construct a new myth, a new view of problems and [a] resolution that is minimally constrained by past myths."[32] In contrast to structural therapists, who assume that the client's complaints are a reflection of some deeper underlying problem, constructivists do not assume a pathology- or disease-oriented view. Instead, they focus on problem-solving behaviors, and they believe that if the client can see things differently, he can behave differently.

Berg used this solution-oriented, constructive approach with Carl, over-looking his "dark cloud" of mixed emotions to inquire instead about his competent actions. After empathetically hearing Carl's detailed account of his suicide attempt, Berg asks:

BERG: Okay. So, how did you manage to get to school today?

CARL: Well, that's a long story, too.

BERG: What a night . . . I mean it was a terrible night you had.

CARL: Way terrible night.

BERG: How did you show up in school on time?[33]

Berg's question about Carl's timely arrival at school is not meant to trivialize his confluence of feelings. Instead, it targets his strengths and suggests that in spite of his previous struggles, he overcame difficulties and engaged in certain competent actions to make it to school. De Shazer, Berg, and their colleagues have devised a number of constructivist techniques that move beyond past problems and navigate language traps.

Beyond Language Traps: The Philosophy of Artful Seeing

In chapter 3, I examined Brian Blount's multivalent and sociolinguistic approach to textual interpretation. In this outlook, there is no singular, correct meaning of a text, but instead textual meaning is fluid and multivalent.[34] Moreover, to achieve a fuller understanding of any given text, both dominant and marginal interpretations must be considered. Additionally, Blount's focus on sociolinguistic theory establishes that textual meaning has both social and cultural contexts. Though Blount's primary focus of study is that of written biblical texts, it involves no great stretch to imagine the spoken word as being similarly multivalent and possessing many meanings of its own.[35] Recognizing the richness of multivalent interpretation in therapeutic conversation, de Shazer uses the contemporary philosophy of Ludwig Wittgenstein to examine "how therapy works within language and how language works within therapy."[36]

Language Traps and Conversational Danger Points

In a coauthored article entitled "Doing Therapy: A Post-Structural Revision," de Shazer and Berg reason that the meanings of words and sentences differ according to a person's past history and present context. On the one hand, "words are like freight engines that are pulling boxcars behind them filled with all their previous meanings."[37] On the other hand, they are constantly changing based on context, such that in each different setting a word's meaning changes ever so slightly, as well as with the passage of time. Because of this, de Shazer explains, "order and understanding [are] only possible in limited constrained situations."[38] Take, for instance, Carl's use of the word *love* as one of the emotions in his dark cloud. With this particular use, he brings all of his previous meanings to the therapeutic conversation (i.e., loving his Aunt Jasper, who sat idly by; loving his brother when they were young children; and so on). But, based on the present conversation of surviving a suicide attempt, he begins to appreciate the support afforded by persons at his school and to realize that he loves to learn. In a different context, *love* takes on a different meaning for Carl.

Misunderstanding Carl's meaning of love, hate, or any other significant emotion presented in a care-giving moment can create a trap for even the best of therapists. De Shazer explains that he is interested in the philosophy of Ludwig Wittgenstein because his ideas acknowledge the traps inherent in language. In speaking of language's unforeseen paths and potential pitfalls, Wittgenstein states:

> Language sets everyone the same traps; it is an immense network of easily accessible wrong turnings. And so we watch one man after another walking down the same paths and we know in advance where he will branch off, where he will walk straight on without noticing the side turnings, etc. What I have to do then is erect *signposts* at all the junctions where there are wrong turnings so as to help people pass the danger points.[39]

One way that care-giving historians can erect signposts to guide clients around wrong turnings and danger points is to acknowledge and identify the "language games" at play in the conversation.

Language Games and the Art of Seeing

Steve de Shazer views therapy "as an example of an activity involving a set of related but distinct 'language games.'"[40] According to Wittgenstein, "language games" represent a communication system that orders life. More specifically:

> A language game is an activity seen as a language complete in itself, a complete system of human communication. Language games are complete in the sense that, you've got what you've got and that's all there is. There is no need to look behind or beneath since everything you need is readily available and open to view.[41]

For de Shazer, "language games" are culturally shared and structured activities (such as words, gestures, and facial expressions) that shape how people use language to describe, explain, or justify. These activities create a unique meaning within a particular relational context, such that particular signs may only be understood within the present context generated between the participants in dialogue.[42] De Shazer describes the shared context of meaning that arises in therapy as a language game that requires adopting an artful approach of seeing subtle differences in stories:

> In the language game of therapy, the client's story makes the therapist see things one way; the therapist's revision (a difference) makes the client see things another way. If therapist and client cannot work it out, if they cannot put the difference to work, they are not negotiating; they are simply reacting to each other rather than replying. . . . In any particular conversation that therapists and clients have, there are many possible points where a distinction can be marked, places where the difference can be pointed to. Any of these differences might be put to work toward making a difference so that the client can say that his or her life is more satisfactory.[43]

The key to searching for differences, distinctions, or clearings is the therapist's ability to appreciate the client's unique interpretation of the story. De Shazer refers to this process of appreciating and affirming the client's unique interpretation, yet seeing and presenting something different, as the "binocular theory of change."

The binocular theory uses the metaphor of depth perception to exemplify how new meaning can be derived when the ideas of the client and therapist map together.[44] De Shazer believes that depth perception is a useful metaphor for therapy because when viewing the depth of an object, the right eye sees something slightly different from what the left eye sees. Neither eye on its own can perceive the depth that the two eyes perceive together. Moreover, if the two eyes are too close or too far apart, depth perception is also limited.[45] De Shazer employs this image to exemplify the delicate balance of collaboration needed between the therapist and the client to *see* new possibilities in the counseling moment:

> In the clinical context, clients describe their situation from their own particular, unique point of view. The therapist listens, always seeing things differently, and *redescribes* what the client describes from a different point of view. A bonus accrues when the two slightly different descriptions (binocularity) are put together. The result is not the therapist's view, but something different from both. But, as with two eyes, if the descriptions are too far apart or too similar, this bonus is lost.[46]

The caregiver has a duty to navigate critical distance and *see things from a perspective slightly different from that of the client.* In pursuit of seeing differently and working to understand clients, de Shazer and his colleagues at the Brief Family Therapy Center realized that they had to alter the power relationships in therapy. To this end, they came to view therapy as an ecosystem in which the once marginalized person in therapy became a central voice of authority and expert of his own story. This boundary-breaking insight emphasized interpersonal negotiation, mutual respect, and seeing things differently to promote change.

Beyond Stalemates: The Philosophy of Redistributing Power

In chapter 3, I turned to Blount's use of sociolinguistics as a medium to understand the frequent stalemates between younger Uth Turn participants and their older, well-intentioned mentors. Blount suggests that stalemates often occur in a conversation between dominant interpretive voices and more marginal interpreters when there is a lack of shared understanding and little appreciation of the other's views. To resolve such stalemates, he advocates viewing dialogue as a "rainbow of potential meaning,"[47] in which a wide range of interpretations is necessary to obtain a fuller spectrum of textual understanding. Thus, one could imagine that if Blount were arranging and mediating a dialogue of dissenting interpreters, he might sit between the dominant and marginal voices, seeking to ensure every party had equal representation in the dialogue.

De Shazer and his colleagues refer to this system of collaborative construction as an "ecosystem." This ecosystemic philosophy states that the caregiver's system (including the team of therapists observing behind the mirror, the video equipment, and so on) influences and is influenced by the family system.[48] SFBT acknowledges that the presence of the therapeutic team—both in the room and behind the mirror—influences the counseling session and shifts the power dynamics in the therapeutic ecosystem. To redirect some of this power back to the counselee the therapists must "lead from behind."

Decidedly different from structural therapeutic approaches, SFBT adopts the position that although therapeutic arrangements are hierarchical, they "tend to be more egalitarian and democratic than authoritarian."[49] As a result, the caregiver, who seeks to see differently, asks questions and makes comments that lead the session from one step behind. In "leading from behind" the caregiver attempts to refrain from interpreting, cajoling, admonishing, or pushing, but instead gently "taps on the shoulder of the client [and points] out different direction[s] to consider."[50]

Berg exemplifies how she functions in the ecosystem and how she gently nudges from behind when she helps Carl discover "the real Carl" who lies behind his "happy face." Consider the transcribed conversation below. (I have italicized phrases in which Carl and Berg developed a shared language pattern. This can be seen in the echoed words and phrases in the conversation.)

CARL: *Yeah,* I know what you're thinking. You're kind of like, well, what is this kid doing here? He seems kind of like a pretty nice guy, but he has all these problems. I usually think of that too, sometimes.

BERG: *Yeah?* What is your answer then? What is your answer to yourself, when you ask that, when you say that to yourself? I wasn't thinking that, but *now that you mention it?*

CARL: *Now that I mention it?*

BERG: *Yeah?*

CARL: I don't know, I think as a person, you know, I'm very sincere. You know, I can cooperate. . . . Sometimes I say, "What am I doing?" That's the bad side. The good side is, "You're getting help," or "You're talking it out."

BERG: Okay. Okay. And, you're saying, that's what helps, here in school?

CARL: Right.

BERG: That's what you like about this school?

CARL: When I'm here I am so comfortable; I'm relaxed.

BERG: You're *calm?*

CARL: I'm *calm.*

BERG: You're *calm* and this is your *real self?*

CARL: This *is my self* right here?

BERG: Coming out.

CARL: Right here.

BERG: In this school?

CARL: Right.

BERG: Okay.

CARL: And then, today earlier with you and me with the discussion . . .

BERG: Yes, that's you.

CARL: That's me.

BERG: That's the real Carl?

CARL: Right.

BERG: I see. And you'd like to see more of those real Carls come out?

CARL: Sometimes.[51]

The above transcription shows Carl and Berg arriving at an understanding of what they see as the "real Carl." This small section of the larger therapeutic interview reveals a great deal about the ecosystemic approach to SFBT and the binocular theory of change.

First, Carl and Berg develop a shared language pattern in which Berg echoes some of the words and phrases in her responses to Carl and vice versa. This is evident not only in the first four lines of the transcribed section, as both Carl and Berg use the terms *yeah* and *now that I mention it,* but also in Berg's use of the word *calm.* Berg introduces the word *calm* to Carl, which suggests that she, as therapist and part of the ecosystem, does influence the conversation.

Although Berg was suggestive in her way of describing Carl, she allowed him the freedom to guide the discussion. Close analysis reveals that Berg followed up on Carl's initial question of "What is this kid doing here?" and she reintroduced school into the conversation, a place that Carl previously stated was "a second home."[52] In this arrangement, in which Berg leads from one step behind, she not only acknowledges the muted voice of Carl and allows him the freedom to determine what and who the "real Carl" is but also highlights an exception that can give Carl hope, namely, that his school is one place where the "real Carl" is calm and the "dark cloud" of mixed emotions is not prevalent. The following section examines how solution-focused techniques such as discovering exceptions can help the unacknowledged envision new possibilities and counter the three primary threats to hope described by Donald Capps.

Practice: Beyond the Snares of Time—The Practice of Reframing and Enlivening Hope

In my first visit at the psychiatric facility with Stephen, the young man who had attempted to take his life by jumping off a bridge, it was evident that conflicting emotions troubled him. We spent a great deal of our initial ninety-minute session talking about his family history and what he perceived to be the factors that led to his suicide attempt. We also talked at length about how he was coping after recovering from the physical injuries that resulted from his failed attempt. Since the attempt, his drug use and criminal activity had escalated, while his severe seizures and headaches continued. Moreover, his one source of joy in life, basketball, was stripped away because the bones in his arm had shattered from the impact of the fall, making him unable even to grasp a ball. He felt incapable of putting the pieces of his body and soul back together. Now, in prison for theft and on twenty-four-hour suicide watch, Stephen was spiraling downward into hopelessness.

Recognizing how reflecting on his past problems heightened his depressed state during our first session, I decided on my second visit to introduce Stephen to a concept called "projective imagination." In an effort to lift his spirits, we framed a scenario during which he was my one-hundred-year-old great-grandfather speaking his last words of wisdom to me from his deathbed. As my great-grandfather, Stephen was responsible for sharing the pivotal moments in his century of living so he could leave me, his great-grandson, with his three most essential life lessons. Willingly accepting this challenge, Stephen spoke to me about how much he admired and had learned from the work ethic of his adoptive father and alternatively how there was a group of people "that want to get you in trouble." As we continued to talk, he came to realize that there was, indeed, a small cohort of individuals who supported him in spite of some poor decisions he had made in his early life. After nearly fifty minutes of talking in character without pause, Stephen offered his final remarks and left me, his great-grandson, with three life lessons: "Live life to the fullest; work on your fundamentals; and be yourself, and don't be like everyone else." Without interpreting his comments, I simply asked him to live his own advice. We prayed and embraced, and he walked out of the room more empowered than when he entered.

As my encounter with Stephen and the previous sections on Berg's work with Carl suggest, Stephen and Carl were haunted by the shadow of death and in need of hopeful, time-altering interventions. In the aftermath of their suicide attempts, time had become a foe and hopelessness an unwelcome bedfellow. The two young men were *despairing* and harbored outward disgust toward friends and family who misunderstood them. They were depressed that they were not fully seen (Stephen, for example, longed to be seen as more than a popular athlete) or heard (evident when Carl cried out to his mother and Aunt Jasper, and neither responded). The cases also suggest that the young men found it difficult to conceive of hopeful futures. Marred by their pasts and bound to the present, they impulsively sought to injure themselves—a characteristic of *apathy*. They likewise felt constricted by *shame* and hindered by failed attempts to better their lot in life. Despite Carl's yearning to accomplish more in life than his brother, a frequently incarcerated gang member, he felt ashamed that his brother brought out the worst in him. Likewise, Stephen confessed in our first sessions that he carried shame into his friendships and familial relationships because he felt that being abandoned by his biological parents made him discardable and valueless. I suggest that the three primary threats to hope can be countered by strategic interventions and techniques employed in SFBT.

Beyond Despair: The Practices of Exception-Finding and Complimenting

As I said in chapter 4, the chief threat to hope is despair or the belief that the future is blocked and one's suffering is without meaning. Despairing individuals often feel disgusted or depressed and have the mind-set that everything around them is negative. In despair, they come to believe that what they want will not happen and that what is realizable for others is not realizable for them. From this problem-focused worldview, it is difficult for despairing persons to envision that they have any tools, skills, or resources to attain their desired goals.

Solution-focused brief therapists seek to dismantle despair by searching for seeds of hope amidst forests of problems. The attentive solution-focused caregiver might uncover these seeds by identifying exceptions to perceived problems and by using genuine compliments to highlight the client's internal strengths. To move despairing clients away from a wholly negative outlook in which problems are dominant, solution-focused brief therapists seek to identify exceptions, those "past experiences in a client's life when a problem might reasonably have been expected to occur but somehow did not."[53] Exceptions provide two pieces of critical information, reframing the perceived limits of time and bolstering the client's hope. *First, exceptions clarify that life is not bad all the time.* If this is the case, despair loses a bit of its stranglehold because the client can no longer view everything around him as negative. Through a focus on exceptions, for example, Stephen could be encouraged to think of times when he did not use drugs or have sex to pick himself up when he felt down. Attending to these overlooked "exceptional" moments of positive action in response to a pressing problem allows the client to recognize the positive alternatives in which he already engages. *Second, exceptions provide clients with a glimpse of the inherent strength they have used to successfully overcome difficulties.* Even if the successes have been few and the difficulties overcome minor, recognition of small accomplishments is hope-engendering. One therapeutic technique used to draw out these strengths is complimenting the client.

Most clients who enter therapy and are struggling under the weight of their problems do not expect to hear a series of affirmations about what they want (in the future) and what they are already doing (in the present) that has proven useful to them. In most instances, despairing clients feel trapped by past mistakes and elusive future options. However, SFBT seeks to shift the problem-focused conceptual frame by offering sincere compliments[54] that not only create hope but also implicitly communicate that solutions are built around the client's exceptions and strengths.[55]

To effectively foster a hopeful environment, compliments must be offered in a way that conveys sincerity and an understanding of the client's issue. They should not be trite comments made out of kindness to the client. Neither should they be offered to make the client feel better about a seemingly hopeless situation. Otherwise, compliments will be perceived as condescending and patronizing and can diminish the rapport necessary for successful therapy.

Sincere compliments pinpoint seeds of hope that the client may have overlooked. Making sincere compliments, then, serves as a tool to stave off despair by bringing to light personal qualities clients can use to resolve difficulties and to have a more satisfying life. In speaking of a client's power to develop solutions, De Jong and Berg explain:

> These qualities—such as resilience in the face of hardships, a sense of humor, an organized mind, a capacity for hard work, a sense of caring toward others, the ability to see things from another's point of view, a willingness to listen to others, an interest in learning more about life and living—are client strengths.[56]

Uncovering clients' strengths is an important mechanism for combating despair because depressed and disgusted persons believe that certain attainable goals are only realizable for others. They have lost sight of their own inherent gifts and resources. This was the case for both Carl and Stephen, one a gifted student and the other an accomplished athlete. Carl spoke Japanese fluently, an uncommon feat for native English-speaking persons. To learn this language, he had to exercise great discipline and put in countless hours of study. Such discipline would prove valuable in helping him learn to remain calm in volatile situations. Likewise, as a highly touted, regionally ranked basketball player, Stephen had to be adept at on-the-court decision-making and leadership to make his other teammates better, both of which qualities translate into off-the-court success. It is not surprising then that in the projective imagining exercise in which Stephen assumed the role of my great-grandfather, he used the basketball term *learning the fundamentals* to convey one of the three life lessons he seeks to pass on to successive generations. For Stephen and Carl, searching through the thicket of problems to uncover clearings of internal strength was vital to zeroing in on a hope that could contest their despair.

Beyond Apathy: The Practices of Scaling and Setting Concrete Goals

Apathy is the immobilizing threat to hope that thwarts desire. Apathetic people care little of what happens around them, to them, or within them. Accompanying this lack of caring is a skewed conception of time, that the future is too far away and not worthy of consideration in the present. As a result, apathetic people may become listless and bored or dangerously impulsive. SFBT attacks the apathetic mind-set by introducing and measuring small, concrete goals that reconfigure time and institute steps to achieve a more substantive future.

Goals are established early in SFBT to help the client and caregiver determine when they will know the problem is solved. This is done at the very outset, sometimes in the very first sentence spoken by the caregiver in a first interview, because, without it, therapy could go on forever. The caregiver might begin a first session, for example, by saying, "How will you know that your coming here to talk with me today has been worth your while?" In working with the client, the therapist tries to elicit smaller, more specific goals rather than larger and more vague ones. De Shazer explains that specific goals that are perceived as difficult but attainable are more likely to be achieved than are more vague, less concrete ones.[57] Accordingly, he believes that framing goals as a solution, rather than as the absence of a problem, is more important than goal specificity. He provides the following example: "It is better to have as a goal, 'We want our son to talk nicer to us'—which would need to be described in greater detail—rather than 'We would like our child not to curse at us.'"[58] In this example, the former intervention is framed positively and is something the son *can* do to better his relationship with his parents. On the other hand, the latter intervention is more negatively framed and takes away the son's agency by merely stating what he is not to do.

These small, specific, solution-oriented goals attack apathy by providing a map, or step-by-step sequence, that empowers the client to attain a goal that otherwise seemed too distant, difficult, or unattainable. Carl's goal was to remain the "real Carl," who was calm and intelligent in the face of adversity. Berg helped him map out this goal by walking him through the sequence of events that happened before the argument escalated with his brother. In this process, Berg helped Carl identify several warning signs that he could use in the future to better handle volatile situations. I employed a similar approach with Stephen, by encouraging him to use the three life lessons as specific goals to pattern his own life; after all, these lessons were his most authentic truths. Though his three lessons could have been more specific, they served as viable solutions to his sense of *not knowing* himself.

In *Clues: Investigating Solutions in Brief Therapy*, de Shazer explains it is possibly more useful to think of mechanisms to measure goal achievement than to set goals themselves. Techniques for measuring success are beneficial, according to de Shazer, because clients are frequently "able to find a way to determine that therapy has been successful and [are] more satisfied when something new or different happens that was not thought of as a possible measure of success."[59] One such technique that solution-focused brief therapists use to measure goals is "scaling."

Unlike most scales that measure according to normative standards, scales in SFBT measure only the client's perception of progress. For instance, in the initial therapeutic session, the therapist may ask the client, "On a scale in which '10' stands for the solution and '0' stands for the starting point, where are you now?" Because the therapist cannot know exactly what the client means by his use of a word or concept, scaling questions forms a bridge to talking about things that are hard to describe. For instance, a client who describes himself as depressed might view not getting out of bed as a "0." However, by virtue of having gone to a therapy session, the client might see himself at the time of the interview as being a "3." The therapist would then inquire into what it would take for the client to make it to "4."

Scaling is a hope-engendering assessment device because it helps the client see his own progress. At the same time, scaling helps the therapist gauge previous solutions and emphasizes positive change. De Shazer explains:

> If the scales go up, and things get better from one session to the next, the therapist compliments the clients, then solicits extensive details describing how the clients were able to make such changes. This not only supports and solidifies the changes, but leads to the obvious nudge to "do more of the same." If things "stay the same," again, the clients can be complimented for maintaining their changes, or for not letting things get worse. "How did you keep it from going down?" the therapist might ask. It is interesting how often this question will lead to a description of changes the client made, in which case again the therapist can compliment and support and encourage more of that change.[60]

Though a scaling exercise was not used in either Carl's or Stephen's case, I found scaling questions, coupled with small, specific goals, to be particularly useful in my work with young men at Uth Turn. For young men who find it difficult to envision hopeful futures, moving toward small goals makes the attainment of future hopes more realizable. Scaling questions allowed these young men to measure progress and celebrate small victories, a key component to the pastoral theological response to muteness and invisibility that I discuss in greater detail in the final chapter.

Beyond Shame: The Practice of Miracle-Making

As previously discussed, shame stems from the realization that one's projected future images were illusions or somehow false. This can lead to an unwillingness to entertain other hopes. For Stephen, feelings of shame and of being unknown to others and to himself were evoked at the edge of the bridge, where his life appeared more illusory and false than real. Two years later, I sought to help counter these feelings of shame by simultaneously pointing him to the future and the past with a technique that is a derivative of an imaginative approach called the "miracle question."

Insoo Kim Berg is credited with creating the miracle question. In her book with Peter De Jong, Berg states that the question is best asked deliberately and dramatically. She suggests that the question should be posed like this:

> Now I want to ask you a strange question. Suppose (pause) that while you are sleeping tonight (pause) a miracle happens. (pause) The miracle is that the problem which brought you here today is solved. (pause) But because you are asleep, you don't know that the miracle has happened. (pause) When you wake up, what would be the first sign to you that things are different, (pause) that a miracle has happened?[61]

Berg believed this structure of questioning was beneficial because it gave clients permission to think about an unlimited range of possibilities. The future orientation conjures up a picture of a time when their problems no longer exist. Berg maintains that by shifting the focus from stressors of the past and troubles of the present to an idealistic, yet plausible world, this imaginative question evokes images of a more satisfying life. This is of central importance for constructivist therapists, who believe that introducing new possibilities can create small changes that lead to more substantial changes. Hence, the solution-oriented belief: "Once they see things differently, they can behave differently."[62]

The future-oriented method that I believe holds the most promise for unacknowledged African American young men, who are traditionally suspicious of counseling, is the "projective imagining" technique. Derived from de Shazer by Finnish psychotherapists Ben Furman and Tapani Ahola, projective imagining is discussed in detail in their book, *Solution Talk: Hosting Therapeutic Conversations*. Unlike de Shazer, who gives little or no attention

131

to a problem's origins, Furman and Ahola believe that the past is integral to solution-building in brief therapy. They contend that when not viewed as an adversary, the past can be "seen as a resource, a store of memories, good and bad, and a source of wisdom emanating from life experience."[63] Thus, for Furman and Ahola, when clients are encouraged to honor the past and learn from their mistakes, projective, therapeutic techniques become even more powerful, and substantive futures can be envisioned.

In Stephen's case, by creating an setting in which Stephen became the expert and bearer of wisdom, I merged solution-focused philosophy with projective imagining. As his caregiver, I led from behind. In the role of my great-grandfather, Stephen was given license to project how his life would unfold. Simultaneously, he looked back on his past to reflect on what he could do differently. For Stephen this was a priceless gift. As one still on suicide watch, he was given freedom to imagine himself as having lived a full and long life.[64] Furman and Ahola contend that this approach of simultaneously moving forward and looking back is useful because it allows the client to reflect on past problems as teaching tools for life:

> There are problems in all societies that are considered shameful to have or to not be able to cope with in the expected way. The mechanisms responsible for perpetuating problems are undoubtedly manifold, but it is certain that both shame and the fear of losing face play pivotal roles in preserving problems and making them worse. . . . The feeling of being regarded as abnormal or inadequate by those whom one is close to prevents people from facing problems and restrains the creativity which might lead to the discovery of solutions. *Seeing problems as learning opportunities, passages of growth, or hardships with an important message, helps in replacement of shame with dignity.*[65]

This rationale had particular import in Stephen's case. Projective imagining allowed him to creatively reconstruct his sense of self as a person who was more than just a basketball player. In that fifty-minutes of role-playing, a pocket of resistance burst into reality, a clearing of hope came into sight, and Stephen grew one step closer to knowing himself. There, he was able to face the shameful moments of his past with dignity and take pride in how the lessons he learned could benefit others. In those few moments, the pain from his past was destigmatized, and, for once, he was given a sense of control over what he perceived to be an unpredictable and intimidating future.

Not only did projective imagining help Stephen view his future more positively but also he gained a greater appreciation for the resources around him. Furman and Ahola believe that giving others something to aspire to not only fosters hope for the future but also changes how people see the past and exist in the present world. In this way, the client is able "to recognize and value progress that [was] already underway, to see other people as allies rather than adversaries, and to think of problems as ordeals that can contribute to the struggle to reach goals."[66] Projective imagining gave Stephen the freedom to envision a more positive future, view his past as a resource, and see the allies presently around him. It is important to note that when countering shame through projective imagining, the therapist must also exercise care in asking the client to revisit the past, so as to not reinvoke the shameful feelings that occurred in the initial trauma.

As Furman and Ahola demonstrate, by using techniques like projective imagining, solution-focused brief therapists are challenged to find redemptive moments or exceptional situations in the client's individual and collective history that bolster hope and garner needed strength for survival. This time-bending phenomenon that appreciates the resources of the past, present, and future is particularly important for African Americans. I believe that drawing upon the collective history of African Americans, who endured psychologically and even thrived despite oppressive systems of slavery, segregation, and life-impinging racism, is just as important as finding strength in one's individual past. Knowing that others have suffered but excelled under similar conditions can generate hope. To neglect this redemptive history of excellence and triumph over adversity is to disconnect the client from an additional powerful resource for overcoming present shame.

A Final Word: Fit to Survive and Die a Good Death

William Gravely's mournful poem "Fit to Survive" recounts a dreadful moment during his freshman year in college when he looked death squarely in the eye and did not cringe. On a mild, late night in September, the eighteen-year-old Gravely left his dormitory to visit friends at a neighboring school. Walking leisurely in his flip-flops, knee-high socks, and basketball shorts, he took a shortcut through an alley behind the campus cafeteria. Abruptly, two men emerged from the darkness, threw him against a fence, and planted his face against the metal railing. Unscathed in the scuffle, Gravely then felt two guns jabbed into his back. "Empty your pockets," one of the faceless voices shouted. Gravely figured that if they had really intended to shoot him, they would have already done so. In his mind the two were "soft" and cowardly, so he retorted, "If you want it, you empty them." They rifled through his pockets, took some loose change, and ran off. Enraged, the weaponless Gravely chased behind the pistol-toting robbers in his flip-flops.

As he recounted this incident, Gravely shared that in all his adolescent years of running the streets, he had never left home without multiple weapons to defend himself or tightly laced sneakers to flee the scene. Ironically, on the evening he was accosted, Gravely was unarmed and was wearing unsuitable shoes for running. Hours later, when the adrenaline had waned and the rage had subsided, Gravely sat in the confines of his dorm and called his parents. In the company of their supportive voices, he began to ponder the value of life and the shadow of death trailing him.

Fittingly, having survived near-death encounters, Gravely, Stephen, and Carl were left to ponder the value of their existence, the fullness of life, and what it might be like to die a good death. Unlike the shadow of death, a "good death," according to Howard Thurman, is not gruesome, morbid, grim, or foreboding. Instead, a good death is a "trumpet call to human dignity" and a deliberate instrument to transcend the boundaries and horizons of daily challenges.[67] To imagine a good death is to claim the power of life and grasp the clearings of hope in the present moment.

On his bedside, and in the community of his parents, Gravely saw the broadening horizons of a good death, one in which he could learn from his past and maximize the educational opportunities in his present. Following the school assembly, and in the company of Berg, Carl shed the shadow of death and peeled away the mask of his "happy face" to reveal the "real Carl." Even in the confines of the county jail's psychiatric facility, Stephen found accountability in the fictive presence of his great-grandson and envisioned a good death long beyond his days of incarceration. Realizing the possibility of a good death in a shadow-cast valley is indeed a miraculous solution that generates hope; a hope only sustained in a community of reliable others.

When Hope Unborn Survived

I'm scared out of my mind, am I crazy then?

To risk pushing forward and change the wind

There have only been minor changes to the
outer man

Metamorphosis; divine pillars hold the change
within

With the same eyes, and a changed mind . . .
hope, I can see again

—William K. Gravely

THE DEATH OF BELONGING AND THE LIFE-GIVING COMMUNITY OF RELIABLE OTHERS

A Letter to My Son on the One Hundred Forty-Eighth Anniversary of the Emancipation

01 January 2011
Atlanta, Georgia

Dear Gregory:

I have lost count of how many times I have started this letter and hit delete. Surrounded by the quiet of the midnight hour, I choke back tears as I think of the words I must share. In grade school, when asked what I wanted to be when I grew up, I answered, "A grandfather." Even then I understood the gift of time, the pursuit of wisdom, and the fragility of life. But in my thirty-third year, mortality hangs heavy on my leaves. The fact is, Son, I may never have the opportunity to pen my memoir of lessons learned or to share with you and your sister, in print, how the very sight of your face fills me with hope for our future. So in these few pages, I scatter my seeds.

You are more than my namesake. We are kindred spirits, always have been. You are nearly four now, but we've talked for almost five years. After learning of your conception, for nine months I placed one hand on your mother's belly and ended each day by reading you excerpts of speeches and sermons from Dr. Benjamin Elijah Mays's *Disturbed about Man*. (Your mother told me you were most active during these late-night conversations). Though Mays's book begins with his riveting eulogy of Dr. Martin Luther King, Jr., his sermon, "The Unattainable Goal," emerged as my favorite:

It must be borne in mind that the tragedy in life doesn't lie in not reaching your goal. The tragedy lies in having no goal to reach. It isn't a calamity to die with dreams unfulfilled, but it is a calamity not to dream. It is not a disaster to be unable to capture your ideal, but it is a disaster to have no ideal to capture. It is not a disgrace not to reach the stars, but it is a disgrace to have no stars to reach for. Not failure, but low aim, is sin.[1]

Do not be surprised, in reading this, if these words reverberate like a tuning fork at your core. They are the pitch from which your life's song is cast. For months, I repeated these words night after night hoping they would somehow take root in you. I believed Mays's challenge and my prayers would give you a fundament of hope to interrupt the shadow of death.

My hopes for your future are fraught with unease, not because of anything you will do; you are the hope of ages past. I shudder at the reality that at some point in your life your hope will be threatened, and you will struggle with yourself and others to have your ideas and humanity recognized. To be sure, I laud the advances of the people of the Diaspora and the fact that in the first years of your life, growing up on the hills of Atlanta, you could gaze at a billowing red, white, and blue banner and call it the Obama flag. Even so, I am not blind to the cultural forces that will seek to cut you dead before you get your crack at life. So, Son, I pray incessantly for brighter horizons, and at the height of my unease, I am comforted by an abiding faith that in my absence, I might entrust you into the hands of a community of reliable others.

In this community, let them see your face; you be their mirror. Soften their hearts with your warm embrace. Look them in the eye, own your name, and be assured that you are the manifestation of ancestral prayers. Love your mother, your sister, and your sister's sisters and realize you need them as much as they need you. Most of all, find your peace in the Reliable Other.

My heart swells knowing that the fearless dialogues sparked by this book might enliven possibilities for you and seed hopes that might bloom in your great-grandchildren. I am most honored to risk personal and professional castigation in this pursuit for you. I love you, Gregory. God bless you and Godspeed.

Your father,

Gregory

I give thanks for the opportunity to wet my quill and share my thoughts with my son and the many unnamed Gregorys for whom I work and lift my prayers. Though this letter was born out of immutable love, I have been forewarned that sharing such a deeply intimate correspondence could incite unwarranted negativity for my family and me. I pray this is not the case. But, with consent from my wife and prayers for the goodwill of those whom I hold dearest, I pressed for its uncensored publication. Transformation of self and others involves risks—a central element to catalyzing change. Under duress, I have found the fruit of hope is not always energizing and may not emerge as expected, but at times these fruits are beleaguering and strange. I am not the first impassioned caregiver to feel the discords of hope. In fact, I have come to find solace in the falling tears and gut-wrenching moans of an often unacknowledged reliable other Lady Day.

In 1939, Billie Holliday released "Strange Fruit," a melancholy blues ballad that likened lynched black bodies to fruit hanging from southern trees on which crows plucked, rain gathered, and the wind sucked. The song's ominous lyrics hung heavy on Holliday, and singing them drained her emotionally, made her physically sick, and reminded her of her father's death. More taxing was the fear that singing an inflammatory song in a powder keg of racial tension might lead to her demise. Yet, in the death shadow of Jim Crow, Holliday closed countless performances while spotlighted on a darkened stage with her head bowed and eyes welling with tears, singing what would be her swan song. Even in the face of the threat of physical harm and her own inner turmoil, Holliday sang in solidarity with those under the persecution of segregation. She belted out deep tones of despair to give voice and visibility to muted and invisible people under the yoke of injustice. She cried out in hope that those being cut dead would somehow live. Holliday provides a valiant example of a reliable other who faces risks in hopes of existential change.

This final chapter distills varied themes discussed throughout the book into five counterintuitive strategies that elicit hope and stimulate transformation of self and others.[2] I call these five strategies the strange fruit of hope because they are ripe with paradox and laden with risks. As the community of reliable others is central to generating and sustaining hopes in the lives of the cut dead, I give considered attention to the interdependent, risky, and generative nature of change. Before these summative tasks, I stress the importance of belonging and pay homage to the cut-dead persons who challenged me to stand unflinching under the spotlight and give their stories voice.

The Loss of Belonging

The letter to my son—and the unnamed Gregorys who will read this book—expresses much more than a father's love and concern. Like James Baldwin's note to his nephew in *The Fire Next Time*, my words seek to enlarge a visible and invisible network of support that can buffer against profound attacks on the identity of nameless African American young men.[3] The correspondence challenges a generation of Gregorys to show their faces to the biological and fictive kin encircling them, even if their kin care imperfectly and at a distance. These young men are then encouraged to look to the past and feel the presence of the "sturdy stock" of lettered and unlettered ancestors who prayed and sacrificed so that their progeny might strive for seemingly unattainable goals.[4] In a more complex feat, these Gregorys must gaze into the future and know that their present actions are "for the sake of [their] children and [their] children's children."[5] Perhaps most difficult, I beckon this generation of young men to see the invisible and receive the companionship and guidance of the Reliable Other. By transcending time and space, this letter summons my son and young men of a similar hue to know that when they find themselves cut dead, they are not alone. They belong.

Belonging—the need for membership and acceptance in a specified group or space—is arguably the most essential of the four fundamental human needs discussed in this book. In chapter 1, I referenced how in the wild, maligned animals, who are torn away from the pack, lack vital resources for sustenance. Equally detrimental, these animals lack protection and must fend off attacks alone. Among the human species, affiliate bonds hold equal importance for survival and growth.

Kipling Williams asserts that when one is ostracized or cut dead, intimate connections are imperiled, environments once deemed stable and enduring are perceived as hazardous, and responses to rejection may create further distance.[6] For instance, logic suggests that socially rejected people would seek to restore belonging by taking steps to reestablish relationships or forge new ones. However, "a growing number of laboratory studies finds that social rejection leads to aggression against others—an action that is likely to drive others away rather than bring them closer."[7] In other words, social rejection and a denial of belonging may be a source of the increased aggression that fuels the combustive rage of social dynamite. So, too, a lack of belonging may be part of the reason some of the cut dead harden their exteriors, keep others at bay, and fade into the shadows as social junk. Whether aggressive and explosive or sullen and withdrawn, the socially rejected, who are pushed away from the pack of community, lack vital resources for sustainable living and are more prone to outside attack. Establishment of a community of reliable others, to which the previously cut dead belong, is essential for survival and the flourishing of hope. Before defining the central characteristics of a community of reliable others, I first return to the lives of five of the six young men who comprised the inner circle described in the introduction and whose stories have been chronicled in this book.

The Inner Circle: Five Young Men and the Search for Third Alternatives

The five courageous young men discussed in chapters 3 through 5 were diverse in age, educational attainment, and socioeconomic background. Their stories exemplified the ill effects of muteness and invisibility and the struggle to attain vestiges of hope in seemingly hopeless situations. Two of these five young men were from Uth Turn, and the other three can be described as students from seemingly more promising social circumstances.

Clients from Uth Turn: Nathaniel and Thomas

Having limited education, minimal employment histories, and few positive communal resources of support, the young men from Uth Turn sought counseling assistance to chart out goals for an uncertain future beyond their incarceration. In chapter 3, I recount my "surprise" New Year's Eve counseling session with Nathaniel, who struggled with "keeping faith" in his ability to change, to reflect on the lessons learned from the past year, and to plan for the future. In our time together, Nathaniel offered his scriptural interpretation of the "faithful fisherman" and how, in struggling to "keep faith," he differed from the first-century fisherman. Little did I know that he was concealing a vital part of his identity. Days later, when cornered and virtually unheard by chiding mentors in a group discussion, Nathaniel exploded with his haunting disclosure that he sold his mother drugs to protect his younger siblings.

Thomas, my second client from Uth Turn, entered the conversation in chapter 4. Caught in a vicious cycle of neglect, Thomas sought visibility and voice in a culture of consumption, in which amassing material gains at all costs was predicated on hypermasculine street credibility and "see-me-now" posturing. After only a few sessions, however, I would learn that Thomas sought to escape the stigma of his street name, "Holiday." Attempting to move beyond his past, Thomas desired to attend college, even if it meant risking the loss of friendships or brought the threat of personal harm.

Three Students of Prominence: Art, Carl, and Stephen

The other three young men had achieved a level of prominence in their schools but still found themselves cut dead and threatened by hopelessness. On the other end of the economic and educational spectrum from the incarcerated men at Uth Turn is Art, whose story I chronicle in chapter 4. A promising Princeton student who once relished academic debate and dreamed of himself working in academia, Art recoiled into lethargic apathy and depression after being "muted" and failed by his professor. Chapter 5 tells the stories of two other young men, both "well recognized" in their high schools. The seemingly gregarious Carl excelled academically, spoke Japanese fluently, and prided himself on perfect school attendance. Stephen, a highly touted basketball player, stood out athletically. But neither young man could cope with the paradoxical pressure of being hypervisible but personally and intimately unknown. Both attempted suicide yet miraculously lived to tell their stories.

Life beyond the Initial Study: The Daily Struggle to Hope

As I have shared the stories of these five young men with various audiences, I am frequently asked, "So how did they fare? What became of 'Holiday'? Did Art flunk out of school, or did he regain his confidence, become a stronger student, and graduate?" I am often reluctant to answer these questions for fear of perpetuating the myth that, once acknowledged, the troubled lives of these young men lead inevitably to happy endings. The truth of the matter is that the stories of these young men, and others like them, can never be wrapped up neatly. In fact, the struggle for hope and the quest for acknowledgment of one's humanity and voice is constant and risky. The five young men chronicled in this book embodied this struggle daily and knew the risks of hoping all too well.

After his release, Thomas chose to live in a homeless shelter because he knew that returning to his neighborhood would place him back in an environment in which criminality was expected. Still, he was in Newark and not far from home. Though he enrolled in a local community college and worked two minimum-wage jobs to support his family, he walked the same city streets where he was *still* known as Holiday. While Thomas toted a satchel loaded with books, his enemies and those envious of his change carried loaded guns. In addition to these external threats, Thomas constantly confronted his own temptations, knowing that he could make more money in one hour on the street as Holiday than he would earn in one week at his minimum-wage job as Thomas. In the face of these perils, Thomas was in desperate need of a supportive community to sustain his hopes for transformation. Whether he found it will be discussed later.

Both Art and Stephen also faced considerable risks in rebuilding their broken lives. Art eventually regained a semblance of his former courage to speak out in class; he graduated from Princeton and is now pursuing his doctorate. Even so, he continues to struggle with matters of self-esteem and ponders whether he would respond differently if a future professor chose not to hear him. Stephen, however, continued to experiment with legal and illegal drugs and fluctuated between jobs after being released from prison. After some pronounced life transitions, Stephen has now shifted away from some of his less-desirable habits and has become an attentive father. In all estimations, he seems to be abiding by the wisdom he shared as my imagined great-grandfather.

143

As for Nathaniel and Carl, I have no clue what became of them. If Nathaniel chose not to "keep faith" and not throw the proverbial net on the other side of the boat to change his prospects, it is likely that he found himself in the same situation as a large percentage of Uth Turn men I worked with, who exemplify the explosive disgust of social dynamite. Likewise, if Carl chose his "happy face" over the more authentic "real Carl," his "dark cloud" may have continued to hover and lead him to spiral downward into the depression of social junk. However, if the personal epiphanies I described in chapter 4 have taken root, I entrust their well-being into the hands of the Reliable Other and exercise pedagogical patience that one day change will come for them. I also have reason to believe that for Nathaniel, Carl, and others like them, limitless life opportunities exist beyond the reductionist binaries of social junk and social dynamite. Caregivers might work to find a *third alternative* to interrupt these death-dealing messages, whereby they are neither social dynamite nor social junk but instead "social neophytes."

Social Neophyte: A Third Alternative

Derived from the ancient Greek term *neophytos*, meaning "newly planted," two definitions best describe the characteristics of this third alternative. Though most commonly known by its religious connotation, referring to new converts, *neophyte* also has a scientific meaning. The *Oxford English Dictionary* explains that in botany and ecology, *neophyte* refers to "a plant species that has (relatively) recently been introduced to an area." Consistent with the idea of the pedagogical patience, in which "seeds of hope" are planted in the lives of the unacknowledged, the social neophyte is a new seedling. Whether previously stigmatized as social junk or as social dynamite, the social neophyte discovers a new perspective on life. This perspective interrupts and rechannels earlier disgust or depression into energy for internal and external change, both of which represent the kind of changes necessary to attain a more promising and hopeful future. Such changes demand of the social neophyte a certain degree of courage to face the constant risks that come with hope and change; a newly planted seed cannot live and grow without significant support, nurturing, and cultivation. This leads us to the second relevant definition of a neophyte.

A neophyte is "a person new to a subject or activity; a beginner, a novice." As a novice, a neophyte is much like an apprentice who is placed in a new environment, subject, or activity under the guidance, admonition, training, and support of an individual or group of master craftspeople. Such apprenticeship is vital for social neophytes rooting themselves in new realities because even master craftspeople begin as novices and only achieve master status by learning from gifted others. In our case, the previously unacknowledged neophyte requires a community of those who have come to "master" the art of hope and the craft of change. In my definition of an interrupting hope in chapter 4, I underscore the importance of reliable others, including the Reliable Other—those who display great skill in creating nurturing, "holding environments" and in cultivating the gifts of others. These reliable others function as "masters of hope" who provide support, assure a sense of belonging, and hold the neophyte accountable to the goals fostered by a new outlook on life. These masters do not, however, infantilize the neophyte. Instead, they view the neophyte as the expert of his own story and "lead from behind" in order to cultivate his voice and bring about greater visibility.

In short, the newly planted neophyte must entrust his newly sprouting hope into the hands of known and unknown reliable others, a formidable risk for one who, understandably, lacks trust and has long been unseen and unheard. But what type of caregiver has the capacity to hear, see, and connect with a neophyte who has long been muted, invisible, and mistrusting? What does it mean to be reliable? Can a caregiver be unreliable at times but still work to generate and sustain hope?

The Outer Circle: Common Ground + Reliable Others

The generation of hope is a communal act. In situations in which persons feel some sense of deprivation, images of hope may still emerge from collaborative interchange. One finds an example of hope fostered in community in the case of Thomas, who spent much of his childhood and adolescence incarcerated. Recall that, in a group session with Thomas, I disclosed that I chose not to respond with retaliatory violence following the murder of a high-school friend, but instead I created a peer conflict and mediation program. Thomas invited me into fearless dialogue with the lewd interruption, "That's b***s***!" Several conversations later, Thomas disclosed that his initial response was so strong because he had never met a person who did not respond to violence with further violence. He went on to divulge that though he did not initially trust me, he desired my assistance in escaping the violent life that typified his childhood and adolescence. My response to the death of my high-school friend provided an alternate image that challenged him to think how he might respond differently when (not *if*) presented with a similar situation in the future. In an environment in which violence is reflexive, the stopgap of this image was one seed of hope that inspired movement toward existential change.

History has taught us that, in addition to communities formed by living people, textual communities may also plant seeds of hope that inspire movement toward existential change. The great German theologian of hope, Jurgen Moltmann, recounted that as a World War II prisoner of war to the British, he not only witnessed the collapse of his homeland but also the inward collapse of other prisoners who gave up all hope and sickened to the point of death. Nearly succumbing to the same pressures of hopelessness himself, Moltmann experienced a rebirth of hope after reading the Psalms and New Testament. He admits that the presence of God found in these readings shielded him from the humiliation and despair surrounding him.[8] It is also worthy of note that throughout the ages, music from the Negro spirituals to modern-day rap[9] has functioned as a verbalized textual community that staved off despair, and, more recently, virtual platforms (for example, places of worship in alternate Internet realities such as Second Life) have the potential to create promising images of change and to catalyze transformative action.

In the above examples, dormant hope is resurrected by the presence of a community that alters one's image of life. I refer to these support systems as "a community of reliable others." Though this community of reliable others can be a multitude of hopeful caregivers, it is not necessary for this community to be large, physically tangible (because they can also be textual), or even present in the earliest stages of development. In turn, this "community" may be composed of just one hopeful caregiver accompanied by the Reliable Other. However, to generate and sustain the desire for existential change, and ultimately inspire transformation of self and others, this community must be grounded, fluid, authentic, reflective, and, above all, reliable.

The Common Ground of Hope

In her image-rich text, *Cultivating Wholeness: A Guide to Care and Counseling in Faith Communities,* pastoral psychotherapist Margaret Zipse

Kornfeld provides the metaphor of the caregiver as a gardener commissioned to tend to the groundedness of community. Kornfeld contends that wise gardeners are knowledgeable of the ground that "nurtures, supports, and holds the plants, regardless of the composition of the soil."[10] The ground serves as a metaphor for a community that supports and upholds life. Further refining her metaphor, Kornfeld suggests that though soil (traditions, backgrounds, ethnicities, and so on) differs in appearance and composition, it is community that serves as the common ground. Kornfeld's criteria for establishing a community of healthy ground are pertinent to this study and provide a template for creating nurturing and supportive environments in which newly planted neophytes must belong.

Community as Gracefully Fluid (or Fluidly Graceful)

Drawing on the New Testament's understanding of perfection (*teleiosis*), Kornfeld suggests that thriving communities should always be in a graceful state of becoming. Nearing perfection, but never fully arriving there, such communities are fluid and open to change.[11] Indicative of this willingness to move toward greater fulfillment is a willingness to embrace growth and difference. In such communities, people of diverse background and ideology are not shunned or shamed for their difference. Instead, the community views the presence of difference as an opportunity for growth and learning. For example, Uth Turn mentors trained to build fluid and graceful communities would, rather than chastise Nathaniel, explicitly value Nathaniel and his voice because of its difference. Having his voice valued creates the space in which Nathaniel can recast his future. To meet the needs of these young men, their communities need to be more fluid.

Communities, like the ground, must also expand and contract in order to sustain the life planted in it. Of this fluidity, Kornfeld notes:

> Some [communities] come about spontaneously, others are intentionally formed. Some communities have a long life, others are short-lived. Some grow out of the workplace, some from involvement with a cause. Some are consciously religious; others are not. Although the explicit purpose of the communities may differ, people in them experience something similar. They experience grace.[12]

The fluid communities described above are dynamic, emerge from some common need, and ultimately are gifts of grace. It cannot be overstated that gracious and fluid communities are ideal sites for growth of budding neophytes because they supply the fundamental human need of belonging that is lacking. Communal grounds rich in grace and fluidity provide both a temporarily stable environment and a place where people are concerned for one another's welfare. This altruistic concern and willingness to accommodate differences ensures those who are cut dead that their presence matters.

Community as Authentic Space

Kornfeld suggests that authentic communication tills the ground of healthy communities. Talking is revelatory. In communicative exchange, we share ourselves with others. Talking and being heard is self-revelatory, providing clarity as one's ideas are spoken aloud.[13] Communities provide spaces for us to tell our story, and in "being listened to, we can know more fully who we are."[14] Therefore, if talking is revelatory and identity-forming, then communities who can hear the authentic, uncut stories of others nonjudgmentally have the power to bolster self-esteem and aid in the gestation of hope.

The power of a community who *hears* people into authenticity leads me to ask: How might Art have fared differently if he had felt heard and not scorned by his professor and colleagues? Might Carl not have "cut his throat" had his mother or aunt heard his plaintive cry for help? Just as being seen affirmatively is vital for development, so, too, is being heard within community essential to generating and sustaining hope. However, it is tremendously difficult for people in community, who are graciously open and empathetic, to hear authentic stories and remain unchanged themselves.

Community and the Art of Seeing through Two-Sided Mirrors

In chapter 4, I discussed the power of affirmative mirroring in the genesis of hope in infancy, the first decade, and beyond. The crux of the psychological arguments assessed suggested that affirmative mirroring of others bolstered self-esteem and matured hope. However, it is highly probable that the master of hope sees himself mirrored in the neophyte he affirms.

I noticed almost immediately that I occupied "a different world" than my Uth Turn clients, but hearing their stories of being overlooked forced me to analyze my own repressed rage from being cut dead. Hearing of their odious crimes unearthed haunting violence in my dreams. In an odd way, they became a mirror, a window to my soul to help me see myself more wholly. Their brokenness pointed to my own unresolved tensions and alerted me to the need for counseling to manage the potentially harmful countertransference phenomenon. Thus, as their caregiver, I had to function as a two-sided mirror. I was responsible for seeing my own pungent repressions and filtering their toxic disclosures, while reflecting back love, integrity, and wholeness. Paradoxically, accepting intolerable parts of ourselves opens spaces within community to love those we detest and dismiss. In this regard, mirroring has a humanizing quality.

The Jewish philosopher Martin Buber goes one step further and explains how the mirroring of God can lessen objectification. In Buber's framework, community is visualized as the periphery of a circle. At the center of this circle is God, who makes the human life of community possible. As a centripetal force at the center of community, God draws people into community to see God's face in themselves. By doing so, God's work precipitates self-absorbed and codependent people to view themselves not as alienated and alone but as cast in God's image. Ultimately, it is through the process of seeing God in themselves that they learn to see God in others. Such an appreciative perspective deconstructs cultural forces that dehumanize persons. The once stigmatized other becomes more human when he is cast as a reflection of one's repressed self and as a mirror image of God.[15]

I refer to the reflective practices of introspectively viewing one's repressions and beholding the face of God in oneself and others as the *art of seeing*, an art that fosters love and promotes wholeness. For the caregiver, the art of seeing creates an empathetic perspective that connects the brokenness of humanity in oneself and others with the divine imperative to love one's neighbor as one's self. Furthermore, when the previously cut dead develop the art of seeing themselves as cast in the image of God and feel perceived as whole persons in community, their existence becomes more meaningful, and it becomes possible for them to love themselves.

Reliable Community: Good-Enough Generativity Is Good Enough

Just as communities are not perfect, but strive for human wholeness, reliability is not contingent on any abstract sense of perfect reliability. This reality does not preclude the caregiver from responsibility or concerted action that will encourage movement toward desired existential change in the person for whom care is offered. The idea of the Reliable Other, as I conceive it, is derived from theorists such as Erik Erikson and Donald Capps, who have spoken of the good-enough and affirming presence of a care-giving other as essential to the genesis of hope.

Good-Enough for Me

As previously noted in chapter 4, for both Erikson and Capps, the healthy development and generation of hope occurs early in life and is reliant on the presence of an affirming and good-enough caregiver. In that chapter, I stated my concerns with this concept because some of the young men I worked with had their early lives thwarted by a lack of affirmative mirroring. Such a lack, however, does not limit them to lives of nihilism. On the contrary, I believe that dormant hopes can be resurrected through communities of good-enough reliable others who nurture newly planted social neophytes.

I label these reliable others as good enough[16] because it is not humanly possible or healthy for any caregiver to accept the full brunt of transforming someone else's life. As stated in the first epiphany in chapter 4, it is vital that the caregiver entrust the life of the social neophyte into the hands of known and unknown reliable others and the Reliable Other. Furthermore, reliable others can only function in a good-enough capacity because in the life of a gracious and authentic community, in which people are fully seen, both the caregiver and the neophyte are being made more whole. Evolving wholeness suggests that the caregiver is not perfect, nor is he fully reliable. Like the neophyte, the caregiver, seeing self and others in the two-sided mirror of caring, is also in a state of becoming. A more expansive look at this interdependence and the mutually formative nature of care in the relationship between the reliable others and the social neophyte sheds more light on this complex process.

Why Reliable Others Care

Just as Capps locates the hopeful self in the first stage of life, I believe the template of a community of reliable others, which fosters hope in younger generations, can be found in the seventh stage— generativity versus stagnation—of Erikson's life cycle theory. *Generativity*—a word created by

Erikson's wife, Joan—does not have a definition in many common dictionaries but is akin to the words *generate* and *generative*. The former, *generate*, means "to bring into being; cause to be (to generate hope)," while the latter, *generative*, means "to have the power of producing or originating."[17] From these two definitions one may intuit that generativity is a creative process of producing something that does not yet exist or is not readily apparent. For the purposes of a community of reliable others, generativity is the creative process of resurrecting hope that may be dormant and not readily apparent to the muted and invisible.

The communal focus of creatively working to empower others is present in Erik Erikson's definition of *generativity* in *Childhood and Society*. He explains, "Generativity is primarily the concern in establishing and guiding the next generation, although there are individuals who, through *misfortune* or because of *specific and genuine gifts* in other directions, do not apply this drive to their own offspring."[18] For Erikson, generativity is a developmental milestone of mature adulthood governed by altruistic concern for the care and nurture of others. Close analysis of this definition reveals that the scope of altruism extends beyond parental responsibility and family connections. Accordingly, individuals who have experienced "misfortune" or who "possess specific and genuine gifts" are drawn to generativity-based endeavors beyond care for biological offspring. These two groups of people—those who have experienced misfortune and those with specific and genuine gifts—are vital members of the community of reliable others.

When working with unacknowledged persons who have an extensive history of mistrust, stigmatization, and feelings of hopelessness, the ability to empathize is important. Persons who have experienced the *misfortune* of feeling unacknowledged and have known and overcome the horrors of hopelessness are prime candidates for offering empathetic care to the muted and invisible. Those who have not had such first-hand experiences require *specific* and *genuine gifts* to connect in a meaningful and empathetic way with the unacknowledged.[19]

In my work with the young men at Uth Turn, I fit into both categories. As an African American male, I had experienced in real ways the traumas of being cut dead in public spaces. However, like the Korean-born Insoo Kim Berg and her client, the African American Carl, my clients and I were from different worlds. I was raised in the South, in a middle-class home with two parents, and I was completing my postgraduate education. Many of them were raised in an impoverished area in the Northeast by a single parent and had spent more time behind bars than in school. Because our life experiences were so divergent, specific and genuine gifts were needed to empathetically connect, to *hear* their voices, and to *see* the image of God in these young men who were stigmatized as threats to society. As such, one specific and genuine gift I needed in working with unacknowledged young African American men was my own "need to be needed."

Erikson posits that the human species is a "teaching and learning animal" and the "mature [adult] needs to be needed."[20] By this, he suggests that just as the child needs affirmative mirroring from the adult, the adult has a need to explain important information to younger generations and to be understood. This connection gives the adult a sense of belonging, making the intergenerational process of reflecting on hope both mutual and reciprocal. Just as funerals serve as reminders of one's own mortality, seeing the brokenness in another can encourage one to see the brokenness in one's own self. Similarly, seeing a young person's willingness to change and develop a more hopeful attitude can inspire caregivers to be more attuned to their own hopes. Here it is important to remember that young people are not passive recipients of mirroring or instruction.

In small pocket moments, such as Thomas's disclosure about his reaction to learning a concept foreign to him (refusing to retaliate after violence), and Thomas's desire to change inspired me to work alongside him as he sought transformation. However, in my work with Thomas as a reliable other, I was challenged to take on the risk associated with assisting him in changing his lifestyle, to reflect on my own fears, and to examine the risks associated with pursuing my own life goals. In this regard, I cycled the process of mirroring: the caregiver sees the client; the client sees the need of the caregiver to offer instruction; and the caregiver is forced to see himself. From this vantage point, the caregiver, as a member of the community of reliable others and functioning as both teacher and student, is required to constantly reassess his own hopes in the process of assisting others.

Widening the Circle of Care with an Interrupting Hope

The need to be needed and to offer instruction to succeeding generations is associated with the virtue of care. Care—"a widening concern for what has been generated by love, necessity, or accident"—is a primary duty of the community of reliable others intent on enlivening dormant hopes in the unacknowledged.[21] The widening concern for the "greater fulfillment" of another precipitates the three components of an interrupting hope: naming difficulties, envisioning possibilities, and working proactively toward change. Care is central to each of these areas because they all involve significant risks if not approached with sensitivity and thoughtfulness. Below, I outline the role of the community of reliable others in employing these components of hope with care.

Whatever its size, the community of reliable others must elicit fearless dialogue in order to hear stories from the margins, name difficulties, and extract hopeful elements. To foster fearless dialogue, the reliable other may have to disclose moments of triumph over adversity in his own life. The strategic self-disclosure of the "misfortunate" and/or "genuinely gifted" caregiver has the potential to penetrate the orb of mistrust and build the rapport necessary for authentic truth-sharing. In the fertile ground of authentic sharing, where each communicant is an "expert" of his own story, the caregiver is primed to hear the social and relational complexities that stifle a person's sense of control.

The community of reliable others must also sift through the weeds of hopelessness that stifle self-esteem and the thorns of problem-talk that thwart feelings of a meaningful existence. Recognizing the psychic toxins of despair, apathy, and shame that immobilize the previously unacknowledged in the present moment, the community of reliable others must work to envision new possibilities. Ecosystemic techniques such as leading from behind, scaling, and projective imagining equip the community of reliable others to find miraculous solutions in seemingly hopeless situations.

Finally, this community of reliable others must act prophetically, even subversively, in nurturing and supporting the previously unacknowledged to work toward change. As hopes involve significant risks, reliable others must stand as connected or internal critics readied to support and advise the previously unacknowledged when faced with disappointment and the dangers of change. I recall the importance of acknowledging and affirming the courage of Thomas as he chose to attend a local community college, confront his enemies, and face temptations on his daily walk to campus. While Thomas reaped startling rewards, the formidable risks he and the community of

153

reliable others incurred cannot be overstated. I conclude this book with their story. However, before closing with their courageous story, I outline the wisdom I gleaned on this journey of learning to see myself and others more clearly. These are the strange fruit of hope.

The Strange Fruit of Hope: Five Strategies for Communities to Cultivate Hope

Engaging the theorists and the young men in this project for the past six years has moved me from the paradoxical tension of being cut dead as a student to hypervisible as a professor. This pilgrimage from invisibility to visibility has altered my vocational outlook as writer, scholar, and reliable other. In this fearless and multivalent dialogue I learned from diverse voices, and from them I devised several strategies to contest forces that make African American young men mute and invisible. I call these strategies the strange fruit of hope because, like the epiphanies in chapter 4, they emerged in me like parables, each of them rife with wisdom and counterintuitive power to interrupt the status quo.

Chief among the strange fruit is the importance of creating pocket moments during which *small* changes can eventually produce *radical* outcomes. Through artistic guidance, wisdom, and the support of reliable others, these pocket moments give previously unacknowledged African American young men the freedom to remove their masks, find their authentic selves, and shed stigmatizing labels that harm them. The seeds of hope planted in these pocket moments are born out of the intentional efforts of caregivers who work to create an environment that is multivalent, ecosystemic, future oriented, respectfully confrontational, and fearlessly honest. Below are the five broad-based strategies to vitalize these efforts.

1. The ground is moving even when it appears still. Small changes lead the previously unacknowledged "gradually and gracefully forward to accomplish desired changes in their daily life."[22] Rather than tectonic plates shifting below ground to create quaking changes, small internal shifts (e.g., pocket moments, ordinary or mundane miracles, or moving up the Solution-Focused Brief Therapy scale only one-tenth of a point at a time), can produce life-altering behaviors.

To the outsider, and even to the cut-dead young man himself, miniscule changes may appear almost insignificant. But the caregiver must come to view small changes in a different light. Because altars in the everyday world[23] are sacramental gateways to divine intervention, caregivers must view mundane conversations and ordinary activities as potential moments for pockets of resistance to burst forth into the present moment. Caregivers must see that even in moments when the wind is calm and the ground is settled, subtle shifts are occurring, in them and in the cut dead.

2. There is an art to seeing rainbows, even when dark clouds loom. Creative interpretations facilitate greater understanding of diverse persons and novel ideas that are often relegated to the margins. Remaining cognizant of the culture of mistrust, in which acknowledgment of weaknesses and troubles may create further marginalization, caregivers must creatively capture attention and strategically build rapport. Like skilled artists, caregivers must be intellectually aware of the threats and allies that diminish or uplift those in their care. They must be emotionally differentiated and free from any compulsion to "fit" into either outdated traditions or untested trends. Caregivers must operate with integrity, have the courage to stand alone, and take unpopular positions as advocates for those devoid of visibility and voice.

Artistic media serves as an instrument to creatively navigate critical distances among communities. In my work, I have found that carefully selected music possesses power to interrupt superficial differences and invite divergent groups into fearless dialogue. This book highlights instances when soulful songs by Lil Wayne and Lady Day and moving poems by William Gravely and Langston Hughes were used as resources to articulate elusive feelings and evoke the imagination. As seen in the conversations at Morehouse, journalistic headlines and current events also generate alternative perspectives of the self and the world. The playful art of narration (e.g., miracle questions, projective imagining, and biblical role-playing) can also paint vivid pictures of a more hopeful future in the minds of those who feel hopeless. Care-full uses of art can build bridges and enrich dialogue between marginal and dominant voices.

3. One flower does not make a garden. There is no single way to read or interpret a text, whether that "text" is biblical, historical, or a living human seeking counseling. This project has gathered many voices to exemplify how diversity enriches and better informs one's understanding of an issue, person, or group. As Brian Blount might say, this capacity to hear multiple voices creates a "fuller rainbow of meaning."[24] From this vantage point, caregivers are encouraged to welcome marginal, unfamiliar, and previously muted voices. Though the insights emerging from the margins may not be normative, they do offer a unique perspective that can alter the previous understandings of caregiver and care receiver. However, hearing, appreciating, and learning from these marginal and unfamiliar voices requires an attitude of modesty and humility on the part of the caregiver.

4. An old tree can honor the life of a neophyte seed. The caregiver must learn to honor the "expertise" of persons who view themselves as "non-experts." Steve de Shazer posits that the therapist must "lead from behind" because the client is the expert of his own story. This book has sought to value the client's wisdom, to believe in the client's resiliency and capacity for change, and to view the client's interpretive lens as a path to hope. This deference to the client's expertise is modeled in chapter 3, in which Nathaniel is seen to have become an expert interpreter of biblical texts. In chapter 5, Stephen assumed the role of expert when he shared his wisdom as my great-grandfather. Likewise, Carl, not his counselor, Insoo Kim Berg, identified warning signs to better attempt to control himself in volatile situations. In each of these situations, the caregiver names the inner resiliency in those searching for hope, avoids imposition of any "expert" professional interpretation, and allows the process of transformation to emerge from the client's own wisdom.

5. Dirty hands and dirty thoughts are pathogenic. Gracious and empathetic caregivers ingest a lot of toxic material as they are challenged to confront hopelessness in their clients and simultaneously to face the emerging threats to hope in themselves. Whether aiding clients who lack hope, serving as a bridge between marginal and dominant groups, or taking a stance against one's disciplinary tradition, the caregiver is psychologically vulnerable to heightened anxiety, intense criticism, and the depletion of hope. For well-intentioned caregivers to remain reliable, they must not overlook their own needs, and must conduct self-appraisals and seek the supportive care of reliable others.

I advocate for caregivers to be more intentional about self-care by melding Capps's allies of hope with my own personal epiphanies. These pragmatic strategies aided me in healthily ingesting and processing the toxins of what traditional psychotherapists often call countertransference. The epiphanies discussed in chapter 4 include: trusting in the Changer, responding with pedagogical patience, and adopting a modestly confrontational attitude that demands honesty and transparency in oneself and in the other. Central to the effectiveness of these responses is reliance on a community of reliable others who generate, and are regenerated by, a powerful hope. Their prominence in supporting the generation and sustenance of hope for the cut dead is vital, but the risks of existential change can be exceedingly high.

The Caregiver's Gift: The Sweetness of Strange Fruit

For years I made the proverbial trek from the quiet greenness of Princeton's campus to the white noise of Newark's brick city. With each passing hour, the silences became less deafening and the wheel more of a vocational compass than an alien thing. In the still moments, my questions persisted: How does it feel to be a problem? How do I live between multiple, dueling worlds—the church and the academy, the dominant and the marginal, psychology and religion? Then, "floating up through all the jangling echoes of turbulence" was a sound of another kind, a deeper note, to quiet my tensions.[25]

All around me were generative voices, a widening circle of reliable others who, through misfortune or specific and genuine gifts, thrived in liminal spaces. In the "waiting moment," textual ancestors pushed me toward unattainable goals, and contemporary artists hastened me to keep my feet on the ground. Loved ones urged me not to hide behind words, to speak with intention, and to "die tryin'" to break boundaries like the Reliable Other. In the wake of the Golden Day, I learned to draw inspiration from conversations with brave young people, like the female students at Princeton, who in spite of their own pressing problems and liminality, were hopeful about their futures and eager to embark on liberating journeys of critical introspection. I came to recognize the beauty of barely noticeable tectonic shifts in the hardened cores of the cut dead preparing for new planting as social neophytes.

Since this project began many Mondays ago, I have been gifted with "quiet eyes" and the art of seeing the humanity and divinity in God's people and myself. But perhaps the greatest gift was the one least expected. In my pursuits to draw the cut dead from the shadows and into the light, they heard my voice and deemed it valuable. In seeing my face, though I was from a different world, they saw their own. The unexpected fortune was that the young men who were cut dead seeded hope within me. They saw me gracefully and heard me authentically, at a time when I felt muted and invisible. I was their strange fruit, dangling before them and seeding hope. They probably never knew that they helped me grow. Key among their teachings was the following: when the reliable other and the cut dead enter community and establish rapport with one another, a mutually formative process is triggered that gives greater visibility and voice to both parties.

Even when receiving unanticipated gifts, precautions are necessary. Self-care is vital. To neglect oneself is like watering the cut dead and newly planted social neophytes with the caregiver's unprocessed toxins. The reliable other must also measure risks. The ministry of the boundary-breaking Jesus, the exemplar of reliability, reminds us that in finding new life in others, caregivers risk psychological, social, and physical death. I was blessed to witness such boundary-breaking courage in one community in Newark.

A Final Word: When Hope Unborn Survived

As I stated earlier, after Thomas's release, he chose to live in a homeless shelter rather than return to his neighborhood and be tempted to reenter a life of criminality. As the weeks passed, the lack of stability of homelessness took its toll. The emotional and financial strain of not being able to support himself and care for his family became unbearable. In desperation, Thomas reached out to me for help. Encouraged by his resilience in the face of adversity, I mobilized a community of reliable others to encircle him as he sought to replant himself in more fertile ground.

I explained Thomas's situation to a small congregation in Newark and, fully aware of Thomas's background as "Holiday" and also of his hopes for a new life, they welcomed him. In exchange for Thomas's service as sexton of the parish, he was given a small stipend and lodging in the church. In a number of ways, the relationship was mutually formative. While the congregants showered Thomas with love, hot meals, and words of encouragement, he implicitly challenged them to examine their own hopes as individuals and as a community that does not merely speak of change, but enacts it in the face of risks. And risks they did assume. This particular church in Newark was located in the thick of drug-infested gang territory, an area where Thomas's infamy as "Holiday" was known. Yet, the reward of Thomas's growth outweighed the risk. So, on late nights, church members took him dinners, and in broad daylight, in sight of Thomas's former foes, they drove him around Newark in search of employment.

Thomas credits a great deal of his transformation to the reliability of that community. They were gracious in accepting him just as he was and fluid enough to accept him within their fold, allowing him to grow in authenticity. Most encouraging was that he reclaimed his name. In their eyes, he was Thomas, not Holiday. Their art of seeing Thomas gave him a sense of mooring that elicited feelings of accountability. He did not want to let down those investing in his growth, so he worked tirelessly for the church and his own transformation. Rooted in community, no longer adrift in the world, the newly planted Thomas began to sprout and scatter seeds.[26]

Weeks after his release from Uth Turn, Thomas told me of a conversation that he had with an old friend:

> When I came home, I saw, you know, a twelve-year-old. He had a 40-caliber in his hand, and I said, "Man, wassup? What you doing? Before I got locked up you was going to school and everything. Now you twelve, you gotta gun in your hand?" He was like, "Yeah, man, I gotta protect myself. I gotta make money." I see the drugs in hand, the gun in his pocket . . . So I'm like, "Wassup? What's going on? You wiling right now!" I'm like, "Why you?" 'Cause I knew him. I knew his family. But I can't really tell that little guy nothing 'cause his mother was a crackhead. You know. I mean. You know his mother was doing drugs, and he's like, I need money. You know his mother really never gave him nothing. You know what I'm saying? The only time he had clothes was from people out there who tried to throw clothes away.

So, what becomes of the young man with the gun protruding from his pocket? Will he wear thrown-away clothes and feel discarded like social junk? Will he tote his 40-caliber and holster rage like social dynamite? Will he remain in earshot of a reliable other and undergo the transformation of a social neophyte? Will the seed be planted, or will it be cut dead? Let's hope . . .

NOTES

Introduction

1. Kipling D. Williams, *Ostracism: The Power of Silence* (New York: Guilford Press, 2001), 60–63.

2. James E. Dittes, "The Investigator as an Instrument of Investigation: Some Exploratory Observations on the Complete Researcher," in Donald Capps et. al., *Encounter with Erikson: Historical Interpretation and Religious Biography* (Missoula, MT: Scholars Press, 1977), 347–75.

3. In *Beyond Ontological Blackness*, social ethicist Victor Anderson supports the notion that African American identity in postmodern era must be viewed beyond essentialist categories that reify race. Instead he suggests that "black identities continually reconstituted as African Americans inhabit widely differentiated social spaces" (p. 11). Given the range of experiences and social spaces forming and informing the identities of African American young men, this book draws generously from their diverse stories and worldviews. See Victor Anderson, *Beyond Ontological Blackness: An Essay on African American Religious and Cultural Criticism* (New York: Continuum, 1995).

4. While sexuality is a vital component of African American male identity, none of the young men chronicled explicitly disclosed their sexual orientation. To this end, sexual orientation is not a point of analysis in the case study material. This, however, does not discount the fact that heterosexism and homophobia are pervasive social ills that perpetuate and exacerbate muteness and invisibility in African American young men. I consider the effects of sexual orientation on muteness and invisibility in a coauthored article with Hashim Pipkin entitled "The Dark Night of Rage in a Culture of Nihilism." In this article we examine how repeated denial of visibility and voice in a nihilistic culture heightens a "killing rage" that has the potential for both destruction and empowerment. Careful attention is given to expressions of rage in homophobia and the forms of latent rage internalized in numbers of young

gay African American men. See Gregory C. Ellison II and Hashim Pipkin, "The Dark Night of Rage in a Culture of Nihilism: An Interdisciplinary Examination of Remembered in Faces," *Pastoral Psychology* (January 2013).

5. Williams, *Ostracism*, 60–63.

6. I expand on the symbolic meaning of the "Golden Day" in chapter 2.

1. Cut Dead

1. William James, *The Principles of Psychology* (New York: H. Holt & Company, 1890), 292–93 (italics mine).

2. Howard Thurman, *The Inward Journey* (New York: Harper, 1961), 20.

3. Ralph Ellison, *Invisible Man* (New York: Vintage International, 1995), 3–4.

4. *The Oxford English Reference Dictionary*, ed. Judy Pearsall and Bill Trumble, 2nd ed. (Oxford: Oxford University Press, 1996).

5. John F. Callahan, *Ralph Ellison's Invisible Man: A Casebook* (New York: Oxford University Press, 2004), 42–43.

6. Ronald B. Mincy, *Black Males Left Behind* (Washington, DC: Urban Institute Press, 2006), 250.

7 Ibid.

8. Luo, Michael, "In Job Hunt, College Degree Doesn't Close Racial Gap," *New York Times*, November 30, 2009.

9. Harry J. Holzer, Steven Raphael, and Michael A. Stoll, "How Do Employer Perceptions of Crime and Incarceration Affect the Employment Prospects of Less-Educated Young Black Men?" In *Black Males Left Behind*, edited by Ronald B. Mincy (Washington, DC: Urban Institute Press, 2006), 67, 294.

10. Bruce Western, Vincent Schilradi, and Jason Zidelberg, "Education and Incarceration," The Justice Policy Institute (Washington, DC: 2003): 2–9.

11. Michelle Alexander, "More Black Men Are in Prison Today Than Were Enslaved in 1850," *Huffington Post*, October 13, 2011.

12. Cornel West, *Race Matters* (Boston: Beacon Press, 2001), 119.

13. Kelly Brown Douglas, *Sexuality and the Black Church: A Womanist Perspective* (Maryknoll, NY: Orbis Books, 1999), 40.

14. Rudolph P. Byrd and Beverly Guy-Sheftall, *Traps: African American Men on Gender and Sexuality* (Bloomington: Indiana University Press, 2001), 298.

15. Patricia Morrisroe, *Mapplethorpe: A Biography* (New York: Da Capo Press, 1997), 248, 249–53.

16. Byrd and Guy-Sheftall, *Traps,* 298.

17. John A. Rich, *Wrong Place, Wrong Time: Trauma and Violence in the Lives of Young Black Men. (Baltimore, MD: The John Hopkins University Press, 2009),* 17.

18. *Oxford English Reference Dictionary.*

19. Todd F. Heatherton, *The Social Psychology of Stigma* (New York: Guilford Press, 2000), 3.

20. Ibid., 5.

21. Michelle Alexander, *The New Jim Crow*, reprint ed. (New York: The New Press, 2012), 157.

22. Ibid., 2.

23. Ibid., 194.

24. Ibid, 12–13.

25. Ibid., 159–60.

26. Christian Parenti, *Lockdown America: Police and Prisons in the Age of Crisis* (New York: Verso, 2001), 46.

27. Ibid.

28. Ibid.

29. Ibid.

30. Ibid.

31. Erik H. Erikson, *Identity, Youth, and Crisis* (New York: W.W. Norton, 1968), 140.

32. Ibid., 244.

33. This section on explosive rage is part of a larger forthcoming article coauthored with Hashim Pipkin entitled "The Dark Night of Rage in a Culture of Nihilism: An Interdisciplinary Examination of Remembered Faces," *Pastoral Psychology* (January 2013), see http://link.springer.com/article/10.1007%2Fs11089-013-0514-z#.

34. bell hooks, *Killing Rage: Ending Racism* (New York: H. Holt and Co., 1995), 12.

35. Ibid., 18.

36. Alice Miller, *Breaking Down the Wall of Silence: The Liberating Experience of Facing Painful Truth* (New York: Meridian, 1993), 19–22.

37. For Erik Erikson, how one is recognized by society and perceived in history are central elements in the composition and development of the self. In *Life History and the Historical Moment*, Erikson asserts that "no ego is an island to itself." He explains that the "'socio' part of identity must be accounted for in the communality with which an individual finds himself," suggesting how an individual is shaped by social interaction within community. Likewise, in the first stage of Erikson's life cycle theory, trust versus mistrust, a harmful social environment in which the infant is not given sufficient attention from the parent, can inhibit the child's healthy development. See Erik H. Erikson, *Life History and the Historical Moment* (New York: Norton, 1975), 19–20.

38. Karen Scheib, *Challenging Invisibility: Practices of Care with Older Women* (St. Louis: Chalice Press, 2004).

39. Anderson J. Franklin, *From Brotherhood to Manhood : How Black Men Rescue Their Relationships and Dreams from the Invisibility Syndrome* (New York: Wiley, 2004), 4.

40. Valerie Purdie-Vaughns and Richard P. Eibach, "Intersectional Invisibility: The Distinctive Advantages and Disadvantages of Multiple Subordinate-Group Identities," *Sex Roles* 59, no. 5-6 (2008): 381–83.

41. Kipling D. Williams, *Ostracism: The Power of Silence* (New York: Guilford Press, 2001), 1–2.

42. Ibid., 27–30.

43. Ibid., 64–65.

44. Ibid., 61.

45. Kipling D. Williams, Joseph P. Forgas, and William Von Hippel, eds., *The Social Outcast: Ostracism, Social Exclusion, Rejection, and Bullying* (New York: Psychology Press, 2005), 22. For more information on the necessity of belonging to human flourishing, see Baumeister and Leary, "The need to belong: Desire for interpersonal attachments as a fundamental human motivation," *Psychological Bulletin* 177, no. 3 (1995): 497-529.

46. Williams, *Ostracism*, 61.

47. Williams, Forgas, and Hippel, *The Social Outcast*, 22.

48. Williams, *Ostracism*, 62–63.

49. Ibid., 62

50. Ibid.

51. Ibid., 63.

52. Ellison, *Invisible Man*, 4.

53. Williams, *Ostracism*, 64.

54. Ibid.

55. *The Interrupters*, directed by Steve James (Chicago: *Frontline*, 2011).

56. Ibid.

2. From Golden Days to Ivy Greens: Caring with Marginalized Populations

1. Ralph Ellison, *Invisible Man* (New York: Vintage International, 1995), 99.

2. Ibid., 98.

3. I explain in chapter 5 why the word *problem* is struck through and why representing or conveying a "problem" is a problem itself.

4. I expound on the metaphorical significance of "the Golden Day" later in this chapter.

5. Robert Dykstra, *Images of Pastoral Care: Classic Readings* (St. Louis, MO: Chalice Press, 2005).

6. Gregory C. Ellison II, "From My Center to the Center of All Things: Hourglass Care (Take One)," *Pastoral Psychology* (2010) 59: 747-767.

7. Henri J. M. Nouwen, *Out of Solitude: Three Meditations on the Christian Life* (Notre Dame, IN: Ave Maria Press, 1984), 33–37.

8. Pearl Cleage, *Deals with the Devil: And Other Reasons to Riot* (New York: Ballantine Books, 1993), 4.

9. Ibid., 7.

10. Emmanuel Y. Lartey, *In Living Color: An Intercultural Approach to Pastoral Care and Counseling*, 2nd ed. (London: Jessica Kingsley Publishers, 2003), 171–75.

11. Mari Evans, *A Dark and Splendid Mass* (New York: Harlem River Press, 1992), 20–21.

12. Gregory L. Jones and Stephanie Paulsell, eds., *The Scope of Our Art: The Vocation of the Theological Teacher* (Grand Rapids, MI: Wm. B. Eerdmans Publishing Co., 2001).

13. Ibid., 53.

14. Michael Hurley, *Researching the Margins: Strategies for Ethical and Rigorous Research with Marginalised Communities*, ed. Marian Pitts and Anthony Smith (Basingstroke: Palgrave Macmillan, 2007), 178.]

15. Ibid.

16. Ellison, *Invisible Man*, 80.

17. John W. Creswell, *Research Design: Qualitative, Quantitative, and Mixed Methods Approaches*, 3rd ed. (Thousand Oaks, CA: Sage Publications, 2009), 7.

18. Davydd J. Greenwood and Morten Levin, *Introduction to Action Research: Social Research for Social Change*, 2nd ed. (Thousand Oaks, CA: Sage Publications, 2007), 4.

19. John Swinton and Harriet Mowat, *Practical Theology and Qualitative Research Methods* (London: SCM Press, 2006), 255.

20. For the purposes of this study, the term *intellectual* will be used as bell hooks appropriated it in her essay "Black Women Intellectuals." She contends that an intellectual is someone who trades in ideas to transgress discursive barriers and have a vital bearing on a wider political culture. See bell hooks and Cornel West, *Breaking Bread: Insurgent Black Intellectual Life* (Boston: South End Press, 1991), 152.

21. Edward W. Said, *Representations of the Intellectual: The 1993 Reith Lectures* (London: Vintage, 1996), xvi.

22. Ibid., 60.

23. Ibid., 11.

24. bell hooks furthers this argument—that critical distance and isolation for the advancement of intellectual work is a privilege afforded to those with power (i.e., men in a patriarchal system) and is not necessarily granted to all (i.e., women or minorities). See hooks and West, *Breaking Bread*, 159.

25. Michael Walzer, *Interpretation and Social Criticism* (Cambridge: Harvard University Press, 1987), 61.

26. Ibid., 39.

27. Ibid., 22.

28. Ibid., 65.

29. W. E. B. Du Bois and Eric J. Sundquist, *The Oxford W. E. B. Du Bois Reader* (New York: Oxford University Press, 1996), 101.

30. Cornel West, *The Cornel West Reader* (New York: Basic Civitas Books, 1999), 305.

31. Ibid., 306.

32. Hooks and West, *Breaking Bread*, 149.

33. West, *Cornel West Reader*, 314.

34. David L. Lewis, *W. E. B. Du Bois* (New York: H. Holt and Company, 1993), 281.

3. The DEATH of Control and the BIRTH of Fearless Dialogue

1. To sidestep the stigmatized label of "counselor" within many African American communities, at Uth Turn, I referred to myself as Goal Orientation Consultant. Within this position my primary role was to encourage the young men to look beyond the present moment and to develop strategic plans for the future. I found that forward thinking was a difficult task for some of the young men, who were enticed by instant gratification and thus lived moment to moment. Therefore, to best serve the young men in this community, I employed unique pedagogical techniques (i.e., music, video, and current events) to highlight the benefits of goal-oriented thinking.

2. Beyond my work at Uth Turn, Fearless Dialogues™ has been utilized as a tool to structure community conversations on hot-button issues. These community conversations are based on the following four agreements:

(1) Each person commits to speak candidly and authentically;

(2) Each person is the expert of his or her own story and deserving of respect;

(3) Each person commits to opening his or her mind to inspiration, innovation, and transformation; and

(4) Each person commits to seeking to uncover hope in what is seemingly small and mundane.

Much like prayer, which has a transcendent quality, the four agreements of Fearless Dialogues™ bind together seemingly divergent groups and persons once superficially separated by class, cultural, and generational differences, to adopt alternative perspectives of seeing, hearing, and changing. Guided by the four agreements, these frank discussions promote the uncovering of gifts in persons and places that were previously seen as despairing.

3. John A. Rich, *Wrong Place, Wrong Time: Trauma and Violence in the Lives of Young Black Men* (Baltimore: The Johns Hopkins University Press, 2009), xv.

4. Kipling D. Williams, *Ostracism: The Power of Silence* (New York: Guilford Press, 2001), 62.

5. Philip L. Culbertson, *Counseling Men* (Minneapolis: Fortress Press, 1994), 85.

6. Rich, *Wrong Place, Wrong Time,* 199.

7. Ibid.

8. Brian K. Blount, *Cultural Interpretation: Reorienting New Testament Criticism* (Minneapolis: Augsburg Fortress Publishers, 1995), 4.

9. Ibid.

10. Brian K. Blount, *Go Preach! Mark's Kingdom Message and the Black Church Today* (Maryknoll, N.Y.: Orbis Books, 1998), 40.

11. When Halliday mentions the *interpersonal,* he is referring to how characters in language—be it written or spoken language—engage one another through interpersonal interaction. It is significant to note that Blount extends and nuances Halliday's interpersonal reference to include the reader's interaction with the text. Through this extension, the reader's engagement with the text is a part of the interpersonal area. See analysis of Halliday's work in Blount, *Cultural Interpretation,* 8, 10-11, 39.

12. Halliday explains that for children, there are seven distinct stages that link language's usage and infrastructure. The earliest stage is instrumental in nature and maintains that a child's primary linguistic function is to use language to act upon the environment and get things done. The second stage is regulatory, as the child realizes that the language of others exerts pressure on the child, just as the child's language exerts pressure on others. Similar to the regulatory function, the social interaction stage entails the child's coming to understand that language orients one's social environment. The personal function, which typifies the fourth stage, further structures the child's environment as he or she comes to sense that language is the means by which personal individuality is formed. In the fifth stage, or the heuristic function, the child begins to use language to explore the environment. The sixth stage is the imaginative function, which provides for the child's ability to manufacture a "linguistically created environment." Last, the representational function allows the child to competently transfer vital information. See explanation of Halliday's six stages in Blount, *Cultural Interpretation,* 10.

13. Blount, *Cultural Interpretation,* 11.

14. The Better Brother Series is also referenced as a resource for navigating violent social media in my article "Fantasy as Addition to Reality: An Exploration of Fantasy Aggression and Fantasy Aggrace-ion in Violent Media," *Pastoral Psychology* 61, no. 4, August 2012, 513–530.

15. bell hooks, *Teaching to Transgress: Education as the Practice of Freedom* (New York: Routledge, 1994), 8.

16. Brian K. Blount, Cultural Interpretation: Reorienting New Testament Criticism (Minneapolis: Fortress Press, 1995), 184.

17. Ibid., 183.

18. Ibid., 3.

19. Brian K. Blount, *Can I Get a Witness? Reading Revelation through African American Culture* (Louisville, KY: Westminster John Knox Press, 2005), 12.

20. Ibid., 176.

21. Jürgen Moltmann, *Theology of Hope; On the Ground and the Implications of a Christian Eschatology* (New York: Harper & Row, 1967), 17–19.

22. Blount nuances the readings of kingdom of God scholars such as Albert Ritschl, Walter Rauschenbusch, and Johannes Weiss to come to his understanding of the kingdom. He challenges Rauschenbusch's views of pocket moments as stable, humanly enacted, social realities that break into history from the future to subsume and transform the present realities of communities. Instead, for Blount, pockets of resistance divinely enter the present and distinctively and transiently transform present injustices, but the future changes do not subsume the present realities. In addition, Blount contends that these pockets offer hope by transforming both structures and individuals, unlike Rauschenbusch's theocratic sensibility that primarily transforms the human politic. Finally, like Weiss, he sees these pockets as miraculous works of God that forcibly erupt into the present. However, in contrast with Weiss, Blount believes that these pockets can be enacted through human agency. See Blount, *Go Preach!* 13–18.

23. To be clear, Blount supports an eschatological dualism and not a cosmological one. In the latter, because the present age is wicked and irredeemable, it must be destroyed for a different and better world to emerge. In this construction, God destroys and starts anew. However, Blount's eschatological dualism postulates that divine redemption is possible in the present and that transformation is possible through the efforts of human action and divine intervention. Thus, divine intervention transforms the present age without having to destroy it first. See Blount, *Go Preach!* 68.

24. Blount, *Go Preach!* 33.

25. Ibid.

26. Ibid., 57.

27. Ibid., 7.

28. Ibid., 64.

29. Ibid., 63.

30. Ibid., 114.

31. Ibid.

32. Ibid., 88.

33. Ibid.

34. Ibid., 90.

4. The DEATH of Self-Esteem and the SEED of an Interrupting Hope

1. This is the recounting of an apocalyptic dream I had that seemed so real I had to face my own fears of imminent death. While recording this dream, two verses from the book of Revelations came to mind. Direct quotations in superscripts seven and thirteen respectively are from Revelation 10:1 and 11:19 in the New International Version of the Bible.

2. In compliance with Abingdon publishing standards, expletives have been edited. However, it must be stated that in the context of caregiving situations, I encourage people to speak in their most authentic voice.

3. *Bid* is a term used to identify a period of incarceration. By eighteen years old, Thomas had been incarcerated more than ten times.

4. See developmental psychologist Edward Tronick's still face experiment on Youtube (http://www.youtube.com/watch?v=vmE3NfB_HhE) to witness the detrimental effects of expressionless mirroring.

5. In this chapter, I examine the works of Erik Erikson and Donald Capps, both of whom support the notion of affirmative mirroring for processes of healthy development. However, other notable psychologists such as D. W. Winnicott and Edward Tronick say that the mirroring expressions of others influence how persons see and evaluate worth in themselves.

6. Kipling D. Williams, Joseph P. Forgas, and William Von Hippel, eds., *The Social Outcast: Ostracism, Social Exclusion, Rejection, and Bullying* (New York: Psychology Press, 2005), 175.

7. Kipling D. Williams, *Ostracism: The Power of Silence* (New York: Guilford Press, 2001), 63.

8. Ibid., 79.

9. Ibid.

10. Dr. Gary Slutkin's lecture "Disrupting Violence" can be found at http://vimeo.com/11841675.

11. Ibid.

12. In an interview on Comedy Central's *The Colbert Report* about her work with the violence interrupters, Ameena Matthews likens herself to a human antibody. In the response to the host's suggestion that she see herself as a white blood cell, she comically retorts, "I'd like to say I'm a paper-sack brown blood cell" (Ameena Matthews, interview by Stephen Colbert, *The Colbert Report*, Comedy Central, February 2, 2012).

13. Alex Kotlowitz, "Blocking the Transmission of Violence," *The New York Times Magazine,* May 4, 2008, http://www.nytimes.com/2008/05/04/ magazine/04health-t.html?pagewanted=all (accessed May 11, 2012).

14. *The Interrupters,* directed by Steve James (Chicago: *Frontline,* 2011).

15. The violence interrupters are deemed as credible messengers because many are "former gang members who served time in prison, which gave them greater credibility among current gang members." Nancy Ritter, "Ceasefire: A Public Health Approach to Reduce Shootings and Killings," *NIJ Journal* 264 (November 2009): 21.

16. Nancy Ritter, "Ceasefire: A Public Health Approach to Reduce Shootings and Killings," *NIJ Journal* 264 (November 2009): 22.

17. Henri Nouwen, *Reaching Out: The Three Movements of the Spiritual Life* (Garden City, NY: Image Books, 1986), 31.

18. Ibid.

19. Ibid.

20. Ibid. (italics mine).

21. By psychologists, I am referring specifically to Paul Pruyser, a clinical psychologist, and Donald Capps, a pastoral theologian who devoted a decade of his life to examining hope from a pastoral psychological perspective.

22. Donald Capps, *Agents of Hope: A Pastoral Psychology* (Eugene: Wipf and Stock Publishers, 1995), 60–61.

23. William F. Lynch, *Images of Hope: Imagination as Healer of the Hopeless* (Notre Dame, IN: University of Notre Dame Press, 1974), 56.

24. A dear friend, Sybrina Atwaters, is conducting her dissertation research at Georgia Institute of Technology on the hope-engendering support networks found in sacred cyber-spaces. She specifically examines places of worship in the virtual world of Second Life.

25. Donald Capps, *Agents of Hope,* 1.

26. Erik H. Erikson, "Human Strength and the Cycle of Generations" in Erik H. Erikson, *The Erik Erikson Reader,* ed. Robert Coles (New York: W.W. Norton, 2000).

27. Ibid., 193.

28. Ibid., 93.

29. Capps's long-standing intellectual interest in Erikson has spanned over four decades. He has viewed Erikson's life and work through the lens of religious biography in *Encounter with Erikson* (1977), analyzed Erikson's developmental theory and complementary virtues in *Life Cycle Theory and Pastoral Care* (1983) and *Deadly Sins and Saving Virtues* (1987), and provided an extended psycho-biographical study of Erikson's *Young Man Luther* in *Men, Religion and Melancholia* (1997). Even when Erikson is not central in the study, Capps typically mentions Erikson's theories in most of his works. He makes reference to Erikson, for example, in *Pastoral Care and*

Hermeneutics (1984), *Reframing* (1990), *The Depleted Self* (1992), *The Child's Song* (1995), *Living Stories* (1998), and *Biblical Approaches to Pastoral Counseling* (2003).

30. Donald Capps, *Deadly Sins and Saving Virtues* (Philadelphia: Fortress Press, 1987), 125.

31. Donald Capps, *Agents of Hope: A Pastoral Psychology* (Minneapolis: Fortress Press, 1995), 33.

32. Ibid., 138.

33. Ibid., 139.

34. Ibid., 139–42.

35. Ibid., 176.

36. Donald Capps, *The Decades of Life: A Guide to Human Development* (Louisville, KY: Westminster John Knox Press, 2008), 6.

37. Ibid., 7.

38. Ibid.

39. Capps, *Agents of Hope*, 33.

40. Howard Thurman, *The Inward Journey* (New York: Harper, 1961), 20.

41. Capps, *Agents of Hope*, 77.

42. The unacknowledged young men I refer to here are adolescents and young adults. With *healthy* psychosocial development through Erikson's life cycle model we could expect them to be located, at least, in the identity-versus-identity-confusion stage. However, because these young men lacked the presence and support of affirming caregivers early in their lives, development was arrested. Instead of living within the fifth stage, they tragically remain in the first, grounded dystonically in a complex mistrust. Yet, I am increasingly convinced there are possibilities for hope.

43. Capps, *Agents of Hope*, 98.

44. Ibid., 99–100.

45. Ibid., 100–101.

46. Ibid., 101–5.

47. Ibid., 108.

48. Ibid., 109–10.

49. In *Agents of Hope*, Capps, following F. T. Melges's *Time and the Inner Future* (1982), identifies the second derivative of apathy as sociopathology. On page 119 of *Agents of Hope*, Capps alludes to his misgivings that the term *sociopath* is often attributed to young, urban males by suggesting that older, middle-class, and employed persons can also exhibit sociopathic behavior. However, due to the overwhelmingly negative stigma attached to this term, I choose not to use it as a way to describe muted and invisible persons who seek freedom from such stigmatizing labels. For these purposes, I have substituted the phrase *present-bound impulsive* to describe apathy's second derivative. See Fredrick Town Melges, *Time and the Inner Future: A Temporal Approach to Psychiatric Disorders* (New York: John Wiley and Sons, Inc., 1982).

50. Capps, *Agents of Hope*, 117–18.

51. It is important to note that although Thomas would endanger his life for instant gratification, apathetic persons fail to take the risks necessary to maintain a hopeful attitude. In cases of impulsivity and extreme boredom, the apathetic individual fails to risk envisioning the genuine novelty of attaining a different life in the present. Capps attributes this aversion to an inability to love self, other, and world.

52. Capps, *Agents of Hope*, 123–26.

53. Alex Kotlowitz, "Blocking the Transmission of Violence."

54. American Psychological Association, *APA Dictionary of Psychology*, ed. Gary R. VandenBos (Washington, DC: American Psychological Association, 2007).

55. David G. Benner and Peter C. Hill, *Baker Encyclopedia of Psychology & Counseling*, 2nd ed. (Grand Rapids: Baker Books, 1999), 285.

56. Ibid.

57. Personal conversation with a practicing psychologist who wishes to be anonymous.

58. Capps, *Agents of Hope*, 138.

59. Ibid., 138–46.

60. Ibid., 146.

61. Ibid., 148.

62. Ibid., 149.

63. Ibid.

64. Ibid., 138.

65. Ibid., 156.

66. Ibid., 161.

67. This beautiful, anonymous quote was painted in graffiti on a bridge near my house.

5. The DEATH of Meaningful Existence and the BIRTH of Miraculous Solutions

1. Steve de Shazer, Yvonne M. Dolan, and Harry Korman, *More Than Miracles: The State of the Art of Solution-Focused Brief Therapy* (New York: Haworth Press, 2007), 115. This interview was videotaped and copyrighted by the Brief Family Therapy Center in 2004. The video recording is entitled " 'I Am Glad to Be Alive . . .': Building Solutions with a Suicidal Youth."

2. De Shazer, Dolan, and Korman, *More Than Miracles*, 113.

3. Ibid., 14.

4. Sherry L. Murphy, Jiaquan Xu, and Kenneth D. Kochanek, "Deaths: Preliminary Data for 2010," *National Vital Statistics Reports* 60, no. 4 (2012) 1-51.

According to Murphy, Xu, and Kochanek, the top five leading causes of infant mortality for 2010 were congenital malformations, disorders related to short gestation and low birth weight, sudden infant death syndrome, newborn-affected maternal complications of pregnancy, and accidents (unintentional injuries).

5. Ibid., 9–10.

6. Arialdi M. Miniño, "Mortality among Teenagers Aged 12–19: United States, 1999–2006." *NCHS Data Brief* 37 (May 2010), 1-7.

7. "Leading Causes of Death in Males United States, 2007," CDC Men's Health. http://www.cdc.gov/men/lcod/.

8. Jiaquan Xu, Kenneth D. Kochanek, and Betzida Tejada-Vera, "Deaths: Preliminary Data for 2007," *National Vital Statistics Reports* 58, no. 1 (2009), 1-52.

9. Kipling D. Williams, *Ostracism: The Power of Silence* (New York: Guilford Press, 2001), 63.

10. In "Special Techniques of Hypnotherapy" (1954), Erickson describes hypnotic techniques such as "symptom substitution, transformation, and the induction of corrective emotional response" that he believes aid hypnotized clients in reconceptualizing problems and working toward change (de Shazer, Dolan, and Korman, *More Than Miracles,* 114). De Shazer credits Erickson's hypnotic approach with one of the central tenets of brief therapy, namely, "utilizing what the client brings with him to meet his need in such a way that the client can make a satisfactory life for himself" (p. 6). In addition to Erickson's appropriation of hypnosis as a medium of therapeutic change, Erickson was also a noted teller of "teaching tales" that had no distinct dividing line between story and strategic intervention. Erickson employed teaching tales to "encourage resistance, provide a worse alternative, effect change by communicating in metaphor, encourage a relapse, or elicit a response by frustrating it" (Donald Capps, *Living Stories: Pastoral Counseling in Congregational Context* [Minneapolis, MN: Fortress Press, 1998], 57).

Melding storytelling with the hypnotic power of suggestion became the trademark of Erickson's therapy. Often resisting the temptation to advise, Erickson used storytelling to help clients imaginatively regain control of their lives. With the freedom to improvise within the framework of the story, the client was empowered to envision a better future and construct positive actions in the present. For more on Milton Erickson's hypnotic techniques, see Milton Erickson, "Special Techniques of Hypnotherapy," in *The Collected Papers of Milton H. Erickson on Hypnosis: Vol. 4. Innovative Hypnotherapy,* edited by E.L. Rossi, 149-173. New York: Irvington, 1980. Originally published in *Journal for Clinical and Experimental Hypnosis,* vol. 2, no. 2, 1954.

11. Steve de Shazer, *Keys to Solution in Brief Therapy* (New York: W.W. Norton & Company, 1985), 78.

12. Ibid., 17.

13. Paul Watzlawick, John H. Weakland, and Richard Fisch, *Change: Principles of Problem Formation and Problem Resolution* (New York: Norton, 1974), 95.

14. Ibid., 126.

15. De Shazer, *Keys to Solution in Brief Therapy*, 6.

16. In *Keys to Solution in Brief Therapy* (p. xviii), de Shazer is careful not to take full credit for the development of SFBT's theory and practice, but instead he refers to it as a team effort. He likens his colleagues to members of a football team, in which the quarterback and halfback (most likely he and Berg) get all the press, and the center, guards, and tackles play vital but essentially unsung roles. The other core members of this founding team of therapists were Jim Derks, Marilyn LaCourt, Eve Lipchik, and Elam Nunnally.

17. Ibid., 13.

18. Terry S. Trepper and others, "Steve De Shazer and the Future of Solution-Focused Therapy," *Journal of Marital and Family Therapy* 32, no. 2 (April 2006): 134. [NOTE: There are four authors: Terry S. Trepper, Yvonne Dolan, Eric E. McCollum, and Thorana Nelson.]

19. Eve Lipchik, *Beyond Technique in Solution-Focused Therapy: Working with Emotions and the Therapeutic Relationship* (New York: Guilford Press, 2002), 11.

20. Information taken from www.brief-therapy.org, the official website of the Brief Family Therapy Center.

21. Peter De Jong and Insoo Kim Berg, *Interviewing for Solutions*, 2nd ed. (Pacific Grove, CA: Wadsworth Group, 2002), 104.

22. Steve de Shazer, *Putting Difference to Work* (New York: W.W. Norton and Company, Inc., 1991), 83.

23. Ibid., 85.

24. Ibid.

25. Ibid.

26. De Shazer, *Putting Difference to Work*, 30.

27. Ibid.

28. Ibid. (italics mine).

29. Ibid., 31–32.

30. Ibid., 44.

31. Ibid., 45.

32. Ibid., 53.

33. De Shazer, Dolan, and Korman, *More Than Miracles*, 114.

34. Brian K. Blount, *Cultural Interpretation: Reorienting New Testament Criticism* (Minneapolis: Fortress Press, 1995), 183.

35. De Shazer refers to the varied dynamics of word usage in therapeutic conversation in Steve de Shazer, *Words Were Originally Magic* (New York: W.W. Norton, 1994).

36. Steve de Shazer and Insoo Kim Berg, "Doing Therapy: A Post-Structural Re-Vision," *Journal of Marital and Family Therapy* 18, no. 1 (1992): 71.

37. Ibid., 79.

38. Ibid.

39. De Shazer, Dolan, and Korman, *More Than Miracles*, 108 (italics mine).

40. See de Shazer quote in Capps, *Living Stories*, 127.

41. Ibid.

42. De Shazer, *Putting Difference to Work*, 73.

43. Ibid., 156.

44. Steve de Shazer, *Patterns of Brief Family Therapy: An Ecosystemic Approach* (New York: Guilford Press, 1982), 9.

45. De Shazer, *Putting Difference to Work*, 97.

46. Ibid. (italics mine).

47. Blount, *Cultural Interpretation*, 176.

48. De Shazer, *Patterns of Brief Family Therapy*, 2.

49. De Shazer, Dolan, and Korman, *More Than Miracles*, 3.

50. Ibid., 4.

51. Ibid., 127–28.

52. Ibid., 123.

53. Peter De Jong and Insoo Kim Berg, *Interviewing for Solutions*, 2nd ed. (Pacific Grove, CA: Wadsworth Group, 2002), 104.

54. For more information, see Lipchik, *Beyond Technique in Solution-Focused Therapy*, 61.

55. De Jong and Berg, *Interviewing for Solutions*, 118.

56. Ibid., 34.

57. Steve de Shazer, *Clues: Investigating Solutions in Brief Therapy* (New York, NY: W.W. Norton & Company, 1988), 93.

58. De Shazer, Dolan, and Korman, *More Than Miracles*, 6.

59. De Shazer, *Clues: Investigating Solutions in Brief Therapy*, 93.

60. De Shazer, Dolan, and Korman, *More Than Miracles*, 8.

61. Berg and De Jong, *Interviewing for Solutions*, 87.

62. De Shazer, *Patterns of Brief Family Therapy*, 25.

63. Ben Furman and Tapani Ahola, *Solution Talk: Hosting Therapeutic Conversations* (New York: W.W. Norton, 1992), 18.

64. Donald Capps, who also makes use of Furman and Ahola's work in *Agents of Hope*, references a similar case in *Solution Talk* in which a fifteen-year-old girl in an adolescent psychiatric facility is asked to project herself into the distant future. This future-visioning process assists the young woman in viewing her current situation from a different perspective. See Donald Capps, *Agents of Hope: A Pastoral Psychology* (Minneapolis: Fortress Press, 1995), 168–69.

65. Furman and Ahola, *Solution Talk*, 148, 161 (italics mine).

66. Furman and Ahola, *Solution Talk*, 106.

67. Howard Thurman, *The Inward Journey* (Richmond, IN: Friends United Press, 2007), 24.

6. The DEATH of Belonging and the Life-Giving COMMUNITY of Reliable Others

1. Benjamin E. Mays, *Disturbed about Man* (Richmond: John Knox Press, 1969), 117–22.

2. Portions of this final chapter are revised from a previously published article written for *Pastoral Psychology*. See Gregory C Ellison, "Late Stylin' in an Ill-Fitting Suit: Donald Capps' Artistic Approach to the Hopeful Self and Its Implications for Unacknowledged African American Young Men," *Pastoral Psychology* 58, no. 5–6 (2009): 5–6.

3. James Baldwin, *The Price of the Ticket: Collected Nonfiction, 1948–1985* (New York: St. Martin's/Marek, 1985), 336.

4. Ibid.

5. Ibid., 335.

6. Kipling D. Williams, *Ostracism: The Power of Silence* (New York: Guilford Press, 2001), 61.

7. Kipling D. Williams, Joseph P. Forgas, and William Von Hippel, *The Social Outcast: Ostracism, Social Exclusion, Rejection, and Bullying* (New York, NY: Taylor and Francis Group, 2005), 203.

8. Jürgen Moltmann, *Experiences of God*, 1st American ed. (Philadelphia: Fortress Press, 1980), 6–9.

9. Interpreting life and scripture from the vantage point of oppression, the Negro spiritual genre frequently uplifts the themes of survival and liberation. The songs advocated survival by affirming dignity in a world that was bent on denying it. They also bolstered hope for survival by connecting the enslaved singer to biblical characters who endured similar injustices. However, the spirituals extended beyond metaphysical hope and conveyed to the singer and listener a willingness to push against the boundaries of one's present situation in pursuit of physical justice and freedom. For more information on how the Negro spirituals—and other musical genres like the blues and hip hop—serve as a source of hope to marginalized people, see Brian K. Blount, *Can I Get a Witness?: Reading Revelation through African American Culture*. 1st ed. (Louisville: Westminster John Knox Press, 2005).

10. Margaret Zipse Kornfeld, *Cultivating Wholeness: A Guide to Care and Counseling in Faith Communities* (New York: Continuum, 1998), 17.

11. Ibid., 20.

12. Ibid., 19.

13. Ibid., 21.

14. Ibid.

15. Martin Buber, *I and Thou* (New York, NY: First Scribner Classics, 2000).

16. The term *good enough* is also used by D. W. Winnicott, although in the theoretical frame of object relations theory. Winnicott uses the term when he refers to good-enough mothering and the mother/child dyad in early infancy.

17. Donald Capps, *The Decades of Life: A Guide to Human Development* (Louisville, KY: Westminster John Knox Press, 2008), 124.

18. Erik H. Erikson, *Childhood and Society* (New York: Norton, 1993), 267 (italics mine).

19.Gregory C. Ellison II, "Late Stylin' in an Ill-Fitting Suit: Donald Capps' Artistic Approach to the Hopeful Self and its Implications for Unacknowledged African American Young Men," *Pastoral Psychology* (2009) 58: 486-489.

20. Erik H. Erikson, *Childhood and Society*, 266–67.

21. Robert Coles, ed., *The Erik Erikson Reader* (New York: W.W. Norton & Company, 2000), 204.

22. Steve de Shazer, Yvonne M. Dolan, and Harry Korman, *More Than Miracles: The State of the Art of Solution-Focused Brief Therapy* (New York: Haworth Press, 2007), 2.

23. Barbara Brown Taylor's book *An Altar in the World* has been formative in developing my own sight and sensitivity to mundane activities as potential sites of divine meaning. For more on this approach to the world, see Barbara Brown Taylor, *An Altar in the World: A Geography of Faith* (New York: Harper Collins, 2009).

24. Brian K. Blount, *Cultural Interpretation: Reorienting New Testament Criticism* (Eugene, OR: Wipf & Stock Publishers, 2004), 176.

25. Howard Thurman, "Sound of the Genuine Baccalaureate Speech," Baccalaureate Address at Spelman College, May 4, 1980, in Jo Moore Stewart, ed., *The Spelman Messenger* 96, no. 4 (Summer 1980): 14–15.

26. Howard Thurman, *The Inward Journey* (New York: Harper, 1961), 20.

INDEX